Don't Get Your Undies in a Bunch

EMILY JOANNE HOOVER

Copyright 2022 by Emily Joanne Hoover. All rights reserved.

No part of this book may be reproduced, stored in a retrieval system, or transmitted by any means without the written permission of the author.

ISBN: Paperback: 979-8-218-00798-0

Library of Congress Control Number: 2022909161

Publisher: Atlantis Publishing
             Jacksonville, FL

Printed in the United States of America

To order books, visit the *www.lulu.com* bookstore, Amazon, or other online retailers.

Because of the dynamic nature of the Internet, any web addresses or links contained in this book may have changed since publication and may no longer be valid. The views expressed in this work are solely those of the author and do not necessarily reflect the views of the publisher, and the publisher hereby disclaims any responsibility for them.

Fun Stuff About This Book

This book is the third I have written in a short-story format. For years I have been known for my funny true-life adventures. Finally, someone suggested I put them in a book. As a former teacher, I also have included some ideas to make your life easier as well as what I have learned from magazines and my friends' life lessons.

My books are perfect to be read one short chapter at a time, as an adult bedtime story, or as a book you pick up while you're enjoying your bath and a glass of wine. They are perfect light reads while you are traveling, except if you are behind the wheel.

If you enjoy my writing, how about a review on Amazon? If you do that you are a very special fan! Love you lots!

Kissy, Kissy Kiss-Ups

It pleases me to dedicate this book to two very special women who have made it possible: Leslie Rahberg, who has typed the manuscript numerous times with grace and wit, and Emily Carmain, who I was blessed to have in my life to do the editing. Even though they nagged and nagged to get this done, I appreciate them more than they will ever know.

Thank you, God, for these gals, my family, and fun friends for funny adventures, inspiration, loyalty, friendship, encouragement, and love. I am truly blessed.

What Readers Say

"I was visiting a book store on a recent vacation and the author was present promoting this book. I purchased the book and was laughing out loud on the plane back home! The book consists of many mini-stories and is a hoot! While I was reading ... I could picture myself in similar situations and that just made it all the funnier. That vacation destination is now my home and this past weekend was again visiting the bookstore and ran into the author. We chatted for about fifteen minutes and when I left, my jaws were tight from laughing so much. This book is as funny as the author is in person! Give yourself some comic relief and pick up a copy of this book. It's a book you'll enjoy and will want to share with others. I'm purchasing several copies to share with girlfriends over the holidays!" ~ *A Southern fan*

"When we moved into our new home, one of the first people I met was a lady with big red glasses coming up our driveway carrying a book. She said, 'Hi, I'm Emily but you can call me "old bitch."' She gave me a copy of one of her books. They are like her personality, spunky and funny. You'll laugh out loud with this 87-year-old, but will also be touched by her joy, appreciation of life, and finding the humor in all of it. If you like Erma Bombeck, you'll love Emily's books."
~ *Mary Beth, Florida*

"I gave all 12 of the gals in my bridge group copies of Emily's book, 'I Hate Porta-Potties, Sprinkles and Tight Underwear.' They loved it! Makes a great gift."
~*A Georgia reader*

Table of Contents

Fun Trying Out for *America's Got Talent*	1
Fun Retiring to Florida	7
Fun with Cars and Car Guys	9
Fun Looking Slender	12
Fun with Donna, Harvey, and Irma	13
Fun Making Your Life Richer	19
Fun with Clutter-Busters	21
Fun with Guys I Adore	23
Fun Working in Atlanta	24
Fun Traveling Solo	27
Fun with Florida Doctors	29
Fun with the Carpet Guy	36
Fun Traveling at Eighteen	37
Fun with Flowers	39
Fun with Dog Names	43
Fun with Trick or Treat	48
Fun Speak'n Southern	50
Fun Going to Modeling School	56
Fun with Fashionistas	59
Fun at Party Time	63
Fun with the Mystery Man	67
Fun Getting Lost	71
Fun Being Beautiful	74
Fun Moving Through the Years	77
Fun with Love, Passion and Sex	83
Fun Saving Money	87
Fun Under the Big Top	89
Fun with Dalmatians and Disney	94
Fun with Sex and Underwear	96
Fun with Cat Tails and Tales	99
Fun with House Plans	101
Fun Being a Parent	105
Fun with Old Bags and Purses	107
Fun and Interesting Trip to Ohio, 2019	109
Fun and Funny Memories of Our Sons	111

Fun with Old Dogs and Old Men	118
Fun with Underwear Again	119
Fun with Doctor Fill 'n' Drill	122
Fun with Downsizing	123
Fun with Animals	127
Fun Life Lessons I (How to Make Life Easier As You Age)	130
Fun with Hubby	134
Fun on Mother's Day	134
Fun Being a Bad-Ass	137
Fun with My Sister	138
Fun Favorite Bible Verses and Quotes	146
More Fun with Dr. Good As It Gets	147
Fun in the Kitchen	148
Fun with Vertigo	150
Fun in the Mountains – Vacation 2019	155
Fun Helping You Get a Job	158
Fun with My Paternal Grandparents	159
Fun with My Maternal Grandparents	162
Fun in Cleveland	165
Fun with No Pity Parties	169
Fun Being Silent	171
Fun at a Mountain Villa	173
Fun with Obituaries	175
Fun with Love and Heartbreak	176
Fun with the Carters	179
Fun and Not So Fun in 2020	182
Fun Writing	186
Fun with God, Goodness, and Gratefulness	189
Fun with More Recipes	193
Book Club Discussion Questions	199
Fun Information About *Decorating Isn't a Joke, or Is It?*	200
Fun Decorating – Where to Start?	201
Photos over the Years	203

Fun Trying Out for "America's Got Talent"

In January of 2017, I tried out for "America's Got Talent" as a stand-up comedian. Getting ready to perform requires lots and lots of verbal practice to get your words to flow and the punchline right. I auditioned because I read somewhere that older people need to keep doing things outside their comfort zone. Keep in mind I hadn't done stand-up in about twenty years but was planning to do so in a few months, so why not try out now?

I did not find out about the Jacksonville tryouts until around noon the day before. That afternoon I got Hubby to look it up on the internet. Before I knew it, they sent me my tryout number. I said, "Oh shit, I guess now I'll have to do it!"

The Jacksonville location was about forty miles away. I could take a number of people with me. I only asked Leslie, my very good friend and trusty typist. Frankly, Hubby would have made me nervous. I might have asked a couple more gals but I needed to concentrate and, if time permitted, work on "my bit."

I gave thought to using some of my old jokes but decided at about 10 p.m. to write some new stuff, then spent a couple of hours doing so before I went to sleep. The alarm clock went off around 8 a.m. Then I sat in front in front of my microwave, punching in one minute on the timer—as that is all they allowed. I had three solid jokes—all about guys and *all true-life experiences*.

My appointment was for 3 p.m. Leslie and I arrived about 2:45. The guy at the door checked our IDs, then directed us to another guy who also checked our IDs, and then on to a third guy directing people to get into a very long line (of about one hundred and fifty people). I said to the very sweet middle-aged black guy, "Hey, Hot Chocolate, if I was your grandmother, how would you help me get through this process faster?" He directed me to another line, where I did my grandmother bit again. This time we had chairs.

The young guy I sat next to had been there since 8 a.m. I had been told to sit there until they called my number. Realizing that it would take a long, long, long time, I told Leslie, "I'm going to talk to the guy at the door." (Where everyone was going when their number was called.)

I did the "Hot Chocolate" bit again. It worked, as we were ushered into another area. From there we proceeded up an escalator to yet another sitting area. I sat next to a guy whose talent was singing. He told me he had been there since 10 a.m. He said he couldn't try out as his throat was raw from practicing too much, but he was staying to meet "them."

I said, "You know, the judges aren't here, just producers." Apparently, he thought he would meet the judges. Soon I saw him talk to one of the AGT people and I believe he left.

A thirty-something sweet young AGT guy was taking groups of people about twenty at a time into yet another room, which turned out to be the audition room. I said, "Hey, cutie. I wrote a book and I only have one with me. I will give it to you for your wife if you can get me in faster." He got the book and I got—surprise—a private audition.

The producer was an attractive gal near thirty. I did my bit and afterward told her I had not done stand-up for about twenty years. She asked, "Why now?" I told her I wanted to finish my second book before doing stand-up again but decided to try out.

After doing my bit, I said, "I'm sorry it wasn't more

professional but I didn't know about the auditions until about twenty-four hours ago." I went on to tell her my material was new and not as polished as it is normally would be.

She said the material flowed and I was "fantastic." If I was chosen, I would be working with a producer—possibly herself. I told her I would love working with her. Then she asked me to send her a tape of myself performing in front of an audience.

Writing comedy is not easy, plus stand-up takes lots of practice. Due to the time requirements of going back and forth to Jacksonville clubs and all at the prep it requires, I felt I really didn't have time. I needed to finish my second book, *I Hate Porta-Potties, Sprinkles and Tight Underwear,* and planned to perform stand-up after completing that. Maybe I would try out the next year for AGT or "The Last Comic Standing." I knew I couldn't concentrate on two biggies at one time (writing comedy and finishing the book.) If I perform, I want to be as good as possible. Meantime, I wanted to get my book out. I am not disappointed I wasn't contacted. I did what I wanted to do. I wanted to venture outside my comfort zone and I did it.

My Jokes at the Tryout

I love giving guys a hard time. Recently I noticed a nice-looking middle-aged sheriff who had just gotten a haircut. I said, "Nice haircut!" He beamed—then I added, "Now all you need is a facelift, right?" He grinned.

Maybe it's my age, but suddenly guys are holding doors open for me. I say, "Thanks so much! But who would know just by looking at you that you are that nice?" (FYI: I *always* get a laugh when I say that. Could it be in the delivery or my grin?)

I went to my internist for a checkup. He went over my blood work and while looking at my chart he said, "Are you really eighty-one?"

I told him, "Yes, I am."

He came over and, after looking closely at my face and neck, said, "You look terrific." I said, "Well, sonny, you need to get your eyes examined, and you need a haircut."

He looked surprised, then went on to tell me his wife was out of town and she is the one who tells him when it is time to get a haircut. Is that funny? (FYI: I heard later that the next day he had gotten his hair cut.)

~~~

I hope to have this third book out soon and plan some book signings plus comedy stand-up performances. I also plan to attend the Dalmatian Club of America, a once a year event, this time in Cleveland. Then I plan to get the next book, *Decorating Isn't a Joke—Or Is It?,* completed. In the meantime, I go to chair yoga. (This is more work than you might think.) I hope to start tai chi again. The summer of 2018, I started Silver Sneakers three times a week.

My day usually starts with having breakfast while doing laundry and getting my laughs from "Live with Kelly and Ryan." I fold towels and make phone calls while watching "Kathie Lee and Hoda." I try to laugh a little and keep up with what's going on. I may be doing some exercise and or other house projects. Too soon it is lunchtime. A couple of days a week, Hubby and I go out to eat; otherwise I fix sandwiches. If I don't have anything else going on, I try to catch up on housework. I take breaks to write or make phone calls. Dinner time varies from 6:30 to 8 p.m., a meal I usually prepare. A few times a week Hubby will grill our meat. He cleans up and loads the dishwasher.

After dinner Hubby usually listens to music. Sometimes I join him as we read or chat. Most of the time I watch television and write during commercials or sometimes talk to my girlfriends. For many years, my dog Diva Darling would have her playtime with one of us tossing a toy in the leisure room. Hubby goes to bed early, but Diva and I usually called it a day around 11 to 12 p.m. Sadly, Diva passed in the fall of 2018, about six weeks after my only sister died.

I hate to disappoint you, but the fun in my life primarily happens around town doing normal things like grocery shopping, etc. I belong to a neat newcomers group that has monthly luncheons, which I attend once or twice a year. Sometimes Hubby and I go to a dinner dance. I participate in a book group but not as often as I would like. Sometimes I attend a coffee and chat with friends. Three or four times a year, I try to organize a lunch with longtime friends.

Once a month I like to attend the local artist group; however, I haven't painted much while writing books. I am active in the local writers group, and I try to attend the yearly meeting of the Florida Writers Association in the Orlando area. When possible, I do book signings and have fun meeting new people and catching up with fellow authors. At least once or twice a year, I try to go to book festivals.

I attend a few dog shows a year, but lately there have not been shows near me. I prefer to go when my co-owners are showing dogs that come out of, or back to, Atlantis breeding. I am a mentor to new owners. Dogs that I co-own remember me for years. I like to visit puppies at about six weeks as I love puppy kisses and evaluating new litters connected to Atlantis breeding.

I love hanging out with my family or girlfriends. As cute as my sons were when they were young, I enjoy them *so much more* as bright adults.

What I don't like about my life is having less energy and a few more health care visits. It seems the housework takes longer and cooking is less fun all the time. (I am blessed to be able to get a few hours of household help every couple of weeks.) Unfortunately, I am an untidy person who could easily become one of those hoarders, climbing over papers, magazines and endless catalogs and books I love.

Add to these, I have over fifty years of dog pedigrees and photos plus lots of art supplies; then there is my fabric stash. I keep saying I need to—and do keep trying to—get organized. I have several books on that very subject that I keep picking up to read. With selling our North Carolina home, we have more to put away, and, dear God, it isn't easy with ADD, getting older and wanting to do some home projects. (I painted my baseboards in one room, but with back issues it took me over a week.) Oh yes, when I have time, I read. I have three books I am reading now.

I try to keep my life interesting by having as much fun as possible. Later in life it is harder, as your energy and body slow down. However, life is what you make of it. I appreciate my family and friends more than ever. I thank God every day that I have them! And I thank God for the joy I find in everyday experiences. I also pray that with good nutrition and exercise I can keep good health and—when God wants me—that death is fast and easy. I also pray He keeps Hubby in good shape. and that I go before him. Maybe that is selfish of me.

In the meantime, anyone want to hire a band and have a party? I'm ready to go if you are.

P.S. I did not get invited to do "America's Got Talent," probably because I did not send them a tape as requested. Hope to do some fun readings from my book at local events and a bit of stand-up.

P.P.S. Then came 2020 and Covid "stay home" mandate, and my struggles with vertigo—maybe I'll do sit-on-a-stool comedy.

Fun Retiring to Florida

It is never easy to relocate. Retiring from the North to Florida can be a cultural shock and it won't be easy, baby, but eventually it can be a lot of fun.

Relocating will require getting that old baby boomer out of his recliner and getting him to clean out the garage and basement. (FYI— There are *very seldom* basements in Florida, and you are lucky to get covered parking and small storage area if you go for a condo.)

Think of the fun you'll have going through the stuff in the basement. Where do you start? Maybe going through the musty, dusty photos of relatives you don't remember and pictures of people you never really liked? What will you do with boxes of stuff never unpacked from your last move? Gee, you just found six boxes of the coolest Christmas ornaments. Time for a drink, don't you think?

Hubby will need to part with hundreds of years of *Popular Mechanics* and, lordy, lordy, lordy, all those dusty *Playboy* magazines. What will he do with the snow-blower, riding lawnmower and antique dental instrument his uncle Ted gave him? Do you really think you can get him to part with his vintage Betty Grable picture or his Farrah Fawcett poster?

Lady, I have to tell you it won't be easy parting with those cool high-heeled boots or your pricy winter wardrobe. Oh, my, what do you do with Grandmother's teacup collection or Mom's souvenir spoons? Time for another drink, don't you think?

You've probably heard "you can't take it with you." No one ever saw a U-Haul in front of a funeral home. However, while I was coming home from a book signing one day, I couldn't believe what I saw. It was a small U-Haul parked in front of our local funeral home. I thought it was so funny I almost wet my panties.

Seriously, getting rid of your stuff won't be easy. If you don't become alcoholics or kill each other, you will live to enjoy Florida's more casual, easier lifestyle, where you can be outside having fun. I would like to suggest you don't bring anything you can live without. Now is the time to downsize or divorce—you decide.

Before buying a condo or home in Florida you will want to do some research. South Florida is usually warmer in winter whereas north Florida can get some frost and cold winds off the Atlantic or Gulf. You most certainly won't need those earmuffs or long underwear to warm your skinny, hairy legs.

Think about spending vacation time in your future town or city before you decide. Notice if there are security bars on residential properties. How far are transportation hubs for vacations or a quick trip to see friends or grandchildren? How long would you have to drive to evacuate for hurricanes? I can tell you hurricanes aren't fun, nor to be taken lightly. Time to have another drink, maybe?

If, God forbid, something like death or illness takes one of you out, what would the other person do? Sometimes people return up North, to be close to relatives. Thinking about that, do you think it is time to pick up a glass? Wine maybe? FYI—I limit my intake at most to one or two small glasses, but getting rid of stuff and moving is a trial on any relationship and may require a bit more drinking.

Florida condos and homes usually are decorated in light or bright furniture—often contemporary or white furniture. Ask yourself if you would like a change, as it usually costs really a lot to move your stuff. FYI—Moving 1,155 miles from Florida to Texas cost our son about $15,000 for 16,000 pounds from their four-bedroom home. Are you sure you want to move that heavy piece of antique furniture?

Things to consider before buying: a safe location, reputation of doctors and medical facilities, taxes, insurance, including flood, and yard maintenance. The Florida grass requires supplements as well as pest control. I am not talking about pesky neighbors but the roaches, or as the sweet, polite Southerners say—palmetto bugs. If you or sweetie would require in-home care, count on twice the price that Northerners pay. Florida utilities I have found are much higher than other states. Since most Florida communities have few mom-and-pop restaurants, eating out, especially in tourist areas, costs a lot more.

What about the cost of having Florida fun? For a trip to the beach all you need is sunscreen, sunglasses, drinking water and a towel. Boats and golf memberships are another story. You can save money on clothing and shoes. However, you need to get rid of your nasty toe fungus before donning your new expensive flipflops.

Some of your friends might tease you about moving to the roach-motel state where you move in— and often don't move out until your final "check-out" in a box of some kind. Will you have your body shipped up North so you can take advantage of that lovely cemetery lot you bought at "Final Resting Memorial Gardens" in Hoboken?

Fun with Cars and Car Guys

Recently Hubby decided he was over "The Yellow Submarine," the Camaro he purchased three years ago. I had a love-hate relationship with it. I never liked it, how too low and hard to get in and out of with its large doors; however, I loved it as an art object in our garage! Think of that bright yellow with the black rag convertible top against the light gray garage walls.

For three days, Hubby kind-of drove me crazy. I was going through the second proof of *I Hate Porta-Potties, Sprinkles and Tight Underwear*. Did I mention I was trying to do a bit of pre-fall wardrobe TV shopping, going to Silver Sneakers three times a week, cooking meals, and washing, drying and folding laundry? Add to that I was trying to clean out closets, answering phone calls and dealing with my sister. She repeatedly planned the exact day of her funeral. I kept telling her, God plans that—not you.

Our youngest, a self-proclaimed car expert, called and said he had sent an email about a car three hours away in Lake City, Florida. Hubby wanted a more comfortable car with less miles. This Buick looked like a handsome red four-door car. It had been a demo with about five thousand miles on it. If Hubby was to buy it, he would get the full warranty.

I called the salesman, Keith, in Lake City. We had a fun talk. The salesman asked how much Hubby wanted for his Camaro. Our auto expert had told us the average trade-in value. Reality set in as Hubby wanted about two thousand above the average trade-in price. We set an appointment for the following Saturday around 12:45. Keith wanted to know the VIN number which I gave him. I told him I didn't want to come over there and be disappointed. He said, "No problem."

We stopped and got a taco, arriving about 12:35. I opened my door and my mouth fell open as I saw a guy about sixty. I said, "Hi, are you Keith?"

"I am," he said.

Maybe not in my right mind, I said, "You are uglier than I thought."

He blushed, laughed and said, "Emily, you know how to

kill a deal."

Oh, shit, I thought. I said, "You made my day by blushing!"

He laughed as he showed us "the car." We took it for a drive and liked it. I'm not sure how much he checked out the Camaro, other than the mileage and generally looking it over. I had told him it looked really good and was always kept in the garage. It had about thirty-five thousand miles on it and it was a 2016 model we'd purchased used.

We sat down in his office. We joked around and finally he talked about transfer of title. I said, "We haven't talked about the deal." (He had given me a very fair price on the Buick over the phone.)

"It is the price we discussed over the phone," he said. *Yeah, yeah, yeah!* I was thinking.

While Keith was setting up the radio with Hubby, I was in another office with the guy handling the transferring of our insurance. I was asked for my driver's license and our insurance information.

Soon we were back in Keith's office to complete our transaction, and I was again asked for my driver's license as I was to co-own this new car. I couldn't find it. Keith called his co-worker who had helped me with the insurance update. That guy walked into Keith's office, where he was asked if he had found my insurance card. The guy looked at me and said, "Didn't you put that in your bra?" I checked and there it was! The guys, including Hubby, thought this was *really funny*. They all had the last laugh. We had fun with Keith and he even offered to take us out for steaks. Unfortunately, we didn't have time.

I drove our new car home, which I loved. After all, it is red, very comfortable and handles well.

Keith called us the next day to see how we liked our new

car. I even talked to his wife. I told her how bad I was to her husband. She loved it. We hope to get together maybe at a car show.

I love car guys—don't you?

P.S. Months later I called Keith to ask him if he and his wife might want to meet up at the Amelia Island Concours d'Elegance. We'll see if that happens. Then I asked him if they sold Hubby's "Yellow Submarine," and he said yes, to a young couple. They loved that we left two Camaro yellow baseball caps in it. Keith told them that it had been owned by a celebrity—meaning me. Is that funny or what?

Fun Looking Slender

There are *lots* of articles in January magazines and newspapers on losing weight and getting "fit." Frankly, you can't turn on a New Year's morning television show without them talking about diet and exercise. We all know this will work to make us look and feel better.

But you'd never guess the ways The Old Bitch (me) has found to look slender. I think we should ride around in a huge Infinity SUV like the one our son rented for our Cleveland trip. It was incredible as it was taller than him—and he is six feet six inches tall.

Or you could have a carpenter make and upholster oversized furniture. Remember Lily Tomlin getting up on that huge rocker when doing her "Edith Ann" character?

Another way to look slender is to wear an all-one-color outfit, preferably a dark color. Maybe pants with a longer, loose tunic top. A wedge or high heel will make you look taller and more slender.

If you use those suck-in, suck-up undergarments, you

might shave off ten pounds. It will make those bumps and lumps less noticeable. If your outer garments are too tight or your suck-up undergarments are too tight, you could look like a sausage. Your choice, baby.

If you are going for support and a more slender look, wear support pantyhose too. Wondering does anybody wear those anymore? Or you could go for a big muumuu like Mama Cass or a tent dress in stripes. If you are really heavy you really can't hide it all. Since it is a new year, I am going for a healthier and more toned look. Hear me, God—I need your help as I do love chocolate, Becky's carrot cake, cookies and peppermint ice cream! Meantime, as I struggle trying to cover my big ass with a longer top.

Hey, babe, if you have a big ass, like me, check out your rear view. If you must wear jeans, they should be black or a dark wash with a tunic-length black top to cover up everything we don't want to see. An all black or navy outfit will make you look smaller. Being tall, I can get by with white slacks and a long top, or a little bit shorter top with a jacket.

Fun with Donna, Harvey, and Irma

We were told to stock up on bread, milk, peanut butter and jelly, and canned food, and to fill containers with drinking water. A possible hurricane was heading our way. This was 1960 when Hubby and I, like most Americans, had a black-and-white television, and no bottled water was *ever* stocked on shelves. We were living in a nice new concrete three-bedroom, one-bath, one-car-garage home with terrazzo floors and a white tile roof south of Clearwater,

Florida.

Late afternoon the weather was beautiful and very calm. Then as the winds picked up, the rain pounded harder and harder. We had a couple of flashlights, which came in handy when the power went out. Hubby and I pulled our eighteen-month-old's crib into our bedroom. I remember I had hurt my back lifting our son so I held the big flashlight as Hubby noticed water coming right through our walls. He got a bucket and mop and spent a considerable time mopping up the rainwater. Surprisingly none of our windows broke. We, like everyone else, had taped them in an X pattern. The storm went on for most of the night. Finally, finally, finally, Hurricane Donna passed.

The next morning our front yard and street looked like a small lake. Because of Donna the power was off for several days. Thank you, God, we were fine. There were very few trees in our relatively new subdivision. A couple of days later, everything looked normal except for a few small limbs stacked at the curb. (In those days, builders took all the pine trees down and did not plant any new trees.)

In 2016 Harvey decided to come to our island; however, at the time we were in North Carolina packing up as we had sold our home. We had seen on television that people on our island were asked to evacuate. After the storm we found out from our neighbors that our home was fine, just a few limbs down. Our neighborhood was unharmed. Thank God again! (There had not been a hurricane here since the early 1960s, when one took out a row of beach houses.)

In 2017, when I heard Irma was on the way, I told Hubby we should leave. He didn't want to go until we were *told* to evacuate. I finally told him that Diva the Dalmatian and I were leaving on Thursday. The storm was to hit here over the weekend. I told him the television people suggested that people in the Jacksonville and surrounding areas should leave on Thursday before the roads were packed with the south Florida folks. He wasn't buying it. Again, on Wednesday evening I told Hubby if he wanted to stay here fine, Diva and I would be leaving Thursday afternoon. Finally, our eldest called and invited us to stay with them in Georgia, and suggested we leave ASAP. Hubby agreed.

It is very hard leaving your home not knowing if it will be there when you come back. There is always the big question—what to take. We took enough clothing, our dog, her food and little else. Due to the storm going through south Georgia, our son's power was off for almost two days. However, he and his wife had a couple of generators that kept two refrigerators and a freezer going, plus a couple of lights. Fortunately, we didn't trip over all the cords. Our son has a gas grill so we ate well, as we always do at either son's home. Sidebar: *All* of my family are foodies except me. One of the many burdens I carry.

We didn't leave until 4:30 p.m., arriving in south Georgia about three and a half hours later. Our son had suggested that we come the back way, on the state roads, avoiding I-95 and I-16. Thanks to those who left early and those who chose the expressways, traffic was fairly light.

Hubby had stopped the mail. It was to be delivered again on Wednesday. On Tuesday he started telling me I said we would leave on Wednesday. I told him I did not want to go home until the power was on in our home. Over and over we had this *heated* discussion. Finally, I told him if he wanted to rent a car and drive back sooner—go for it. I would be happy to drop him at the rental dealer. After talking with neighbors and finding out the power wasn't on, he finally got the message. (FYI: It ain't easy staying married.)

I know I'm not easy to live with any time, but can you

imagine inside your home being over ninety degrees, no air, no lights, no television? I would have had been miserable and I believe normally dear sweet Hubby would have been too. I told him *several* times I was not into camping. I said this most of the time in a calm way. I just kept saying, "I'm not leaving here until I know our power's on at home."

Wednesday evening we got a call and our power had been restored—yeah! I may act stupid, but sometimes I am smart. I called a good friend and asked if she would go clean out our freezer and refrigerator and toss everything. Bless her heart, she did. She told me the house was *really hot*. We lost a lot of good stuff in that freezer.

We left Georgia about noon on Thursday, which I think helped us miss a lot of the traffic. I spoke to a friend who got stuck on I-95 and she said it was a mess—two accidents. We also spoke to a neighbor who told us we had *several* trees down and our wooden fence was history, but our house seemed fine. About four hours later we arrived home, and seven trees were down, plus our old fence would have to be replaced. I made several calls to tree removal companies as well as fence people. Days later we hadn't heard from them. Hubby and our sweet neighbor sorta fixed our fence so we could let Diva out without being on a lead. Thank God for great neighbors and for protecting our home.

Finally, we got a knock on the door. It was from our previous tree service. This gal remembered me because she remembered our old Dals, Tex and My My. She gave us a fair estimate and said they could come in three to four weeks. She seemed pleased when I gave her my *Panties* book. She also said if she were me, she would not sleep in my back bedroom as anytime my neighbor's tree could fall on our house. I told her I sometimes live on the edge—so I might. Hubby said he felt the tree wouldn't go over unless it was rainy or windy. I decided to live on the edge and slept in my own bed, thinking in the morning I would move my necessary stuff upstairs to the bonus room. I told Hubby that he might have lost his chance to have me die of natural causes.

The next day we heard from another neighbor that a tree service from Iowa was in town and working in our neighborhood. "Our favorite" long-time neighbor had checked them out and they were insured and would start taking the tree down that was leaning over our house. Did we want to talk to him? "Yes!!!"

Mr. Iowa was a cute thirties guy who had been in the tree business over ten years. He was over six feet, had a small beard, pretty eyes and a probably ripped body! (Hey—I'm not blind.) He was also nice to old people, dogs and seemed to be very good at what he did. He had five or six people doing most the work. They all seemed to get along well and were skilled at what they did. One of the guys had to go up very tall trees to cut limbs off before they took them down. Four worked in our yard from noon until it was dark. I told several of the guys to be sure to use sunscreen and if they got sunburned to use aloe vera. (Florida sun is harsher than Northern sun.)

Mr. Iowa was talking to my neighbor and me and asked if he could come back on Sunday to finish. I said, "Yes, what time do you want to come?" He said, "Eight."

I said, "S_ _ _ d_ _ _ hell no!" He laughed. I said, "Go do our neighbors first, please."

He said, "Okay."

They were here by nine thirty, finishing about four thirty. They hauled all the stuff to the street. We had a fortress. The mess was about fifteen to eighteen feet high and forty to fifty feet wide with a depth of twenty feet sitting on our grass in front. On the other side of the drive was another huge load from our big hickory tree. He estimated it would be over one thousand dollars to haul it away. Thus, we waited on FEMA for twelve weeks. We were up to about nine thousand dollars plus three thousand dollars for a plain wood six-foot-tall fence around our not-huge yard.

Why would anyone want to live here if this happens? Because if you are up North, you can have horrible snowstorm damage, frozen earth, tornadoes and, in some parts of our country, big fires. Every day we open our eyes, things can happen. We feel blessed to live in the sunshine and to be a part of a wonderful community—that's why! Thank you, God!

We could have been without home and power like all those people in Puerto Rico, or the earthquake victims in Mexico or the California and West Coast people who lost their homes due to fires and mudslides.

Almost three months after the storm when FEMA picked up all the mess, we had to have a lot of our grass replaced We also added two palm trees as they normally survive storms. In addition, we had to replace plants. More and more money but, hey, our house was fine and we were okay. A year later our island was back to normal. It is unbelievable how fast grass and plants come back here!

P.S. A cute story: While talking to the Iowa guys, I noticed a "cutie" with a lip ring. In front of his boss, I said to my friendly neighbor who had a lead on his small dog, "If you would loan me your dog lead, I could snap it on this guy's lip and lead him around." Cutie replied, "I'd do it for treats." My advice: Have some fun while dealing with the irritations of life.

P.P.S. My yoga teacher says I should tell you that Hubby and I decided against a vinyl fence and are going for a wood one as our current fence lasted eighteen years. We won't need it to last any longer as we won't be here. She thought that sounded funny and told me to include it in this chapter.

P.P.P.S. Please support the Red Cross.

Fun Making Your Life Richer

George Bernard Shaw, the Irish playwright, said, "Life isn't about finding yourself. Life is about creating yourself." People now call this "branding."

Life isn't always easy, kiddo. Some people seem to have a really hard time, but "rise above it." Recently on television I saw a young man who became valedictorian of his senior class. What made this unusual is that for most of his high school years he was homeless. Not the ideal situation for serious studying, is it?

I have several friends who are now in their late eighties. I have learned a lot from them. It always helps to have some older friends you can go to for advice and inspiration (besides God). And often these people are happy to be your mentor. One of my friends has an older woman doctor friend who taught her in nursing school. This doctor is over one hundred, yet she still writes health and family articles for her local paper.

You can make your life richer by opening your mind by listening to older relatives and friends. Turn off your phone and look at others as they share life experiences.

You might consider getting a book that changed my life years ago. Actually, this is four books in one. I'm not sure when the first book, *The Game of Life,* was published. I first bought this book in the early 1970s. I passed it on when I found her four-in-one book, *The Wisdom of Florence Sconel Shinn.* The four complete books are as follows: *The Game of Life, The Power of the Spoken Word, Your Word Is Your Wand* and *The Secret of Success.* Publishers Simon &

Schuster bought the rights to the books in about 1940.

Florence Sconel Shinn was well known as a metaphysician and lecturer as well as an illustrator and artist. I read she helped thousands of people with solving their problems and a great many with healing.

Dr. Norman Vincent Peale, who was a minister of a very large church in New York in the 1950s, '60s and '70s, said of Florence's book: *"The Game of Life* is filled with wisdom and creative insights. Its teachings will work, I know to be fact, for I've long used them myself." He was as important and well known as Billy Graham later became. They both were ministers to presidents.

Important author Emmet Fox is quoted as saying, "The secret to Florence's success was that she was always herself, colloquial, informal, friendly and humorous. She herself was very spiritual ... and taught by familiar, practical and everyday examples."

I quote Florence Sconel Shinn from *The Game of Life*: "All power is given man upon his earth. I have seen many healings accomplished by using the words, 'In the name of Jesus Christ.'"

She teaches just how powerful your thoughts and works can be. To quote her again, "Man should make an art of thinking. The master thinker (God) is an artist and is careful to paint only the divine designs upon the canvas of his mind: and he paints these pictures with masterly strokes of power and decision, having perfect faith that there is no power to mar their perfection and that they shall manifest in his life the ideal made real."

Ask yourself how you can make your life richer. Then do it, baby!

Fun with Clutter-Busters

I was born with the "clutter gene." Really, it is a "real thing" and it can be inherited. My mother, brother and I all had this problem. It seems one of my sons also suffers from "too much stuff." One of the worst things I deal with in life is seeing my faults seemingly magnified in my kids.

Fortunately, I almost always have a clean house, but since I write my books by hand and have to do so many rewrites, I have a lot of necessary papers. Books, papers and mail have always been difficult for me to deal with as I think, "Oh, I'll read or deal with this later." I go to bed, and I swear the papers have wild crazy sex and have lots of offspring during the night.

The worst of it is I know what to do—I just seem incapable of acting on clutter until it gets out of hand.

What I usually do right is hanging up my clothes after I take them off. I always put my car keys next to our answering machine and my handbag in the same place. Dishes, pots, pans and everyday tableware are put away in "their place." Towels and clothes are put away soon after they come out of the dryer. Okay, sometimes it takes a day or two. Clearly, newspapers, magazines and catalogs own me. However, I keep trying to get organized by reading articles and books to become better at managing my huge problem.

I know I am not alone here. While standing in line to pay for my groceries, I see a lot of women's magazines that seem to have—guess what? Covers that contain "features," or as I call them, "teasers," of articles in the magazine. I have noticed a lot of clutter-control features. So, babe, we aren't alone. If we *don't* want to be hoarders, we *need* to control our clutter problems NOW! Experts say even ten minutes a day goes a long way toward giving you and me an easier life. I am trying to do this every day. I do see some progress.

Note! This could take a while, but nothing ventured, nothing gained. From what I read, we start by stowing items where they need to go while they are still in our hot little hands. Encourage your children to pick up their belongings and put them away.

The next step is to set a timer for ten minutes to sift through a drawer or a pile of papers. If you don't get it all done, start there the next day.

A good hint I read was to only purchase things you need and have storage space to hold, or have a spot in your garage for any back stock.

Clean out and toss anything broken or not needed. Plan on selling or recycling items that have not been used in the last year.

Another great idea is to give items you haven't used—maybe in a year—an expiration date. Do you really have to keep something that you aren't using, don't really love or need? Or is the space better used for something else?

Think about it, and if you aren't sure within sixty seconds, you need to find it a new home. It can be taken to a resale shop, given to someone, given to charity or tossed in the trash. The choice is yours!

Conquer by dividing your stuff into "like kind" items. Pare down by one day sorting through your handbags, then another day your shoes. That way you won't feel so overwhelmed. Continue on your road to an easier-to-keep home by moving out an item for each new thing you buy. Actually, if you take two things out before purchasing, say, a new pair of pants, you will soon have a wonderful workable closet. So they say—I am trying.

If you receive a gift of an item you wouldn't buy and aren't going to use it, pass it on as quickly as possible. To help you decide what to do, ask yourself if this would be something you would purchase. If you find yourself with two of anything, keep one and pass on the extra one. No one needs two ice cream scoops.

When you go to purge your closet, you may need to find an honest yet understanding friend to tell you that those tights make your butt and stomach look big, sister.

At some point you may need to conquer more space by parting with a piece or two of your furniture. This could be the time to redecorate after you see the floor again. I have read that smart people do not buy or keep anything they don't really need or truly love. Now you found out that I could be a LOT brighter.

Now is the time for action at our house. I told Hubby that I am going to be throwing out a lot of stuff. I suggested he could help me or he might be the next to go. Only joking, sweetheart.

Fun with Guys I Adore

I adore Willie Nelson as I am a fan of his music and I admire his raising more than fifty-three million dollars to help American farmers through his Farm Aid project that he founded in 1985.

Then there's Jay Leno—because he is funny and, like me, he appreciates cool cars.

Blake Shelton I adore, because he is tall, good-looking, and he's a smart-ass like me. Bet he gives good hugs like my tall son.

Another guy I adore is LeBron James because he has done wonderful things for his hometown, Akron, Ohio. He also continues to make awesome basketball shots. I hated to see him leave Cleveland but I get it—money, sunshine, and he already had a house in L.A. I heard six months to a year before he moved to the L.A. Lakers that he was seen working out with the guys there. I read that he has done a few walk-on movie bits. He is a very smart guy, to be thinking of the future. His basketball career won't last forever. And he is thirty-five already. Hopefully, the team chemistry will work and LeBron won't lose his fan base, but he did piss off a lot of people by leaving Cleveland. He needs to make his team into a big winning one. I hear that Michael Jordan said he feels LeBron James is the greatest basketball player ever. His footwork is amazing to watch. Now I hear rumors that he isn't all that happy in L.A. He can't win games by himself and his first Lakers' season was disappointing. In the second season they seem to be working better together.

Jimmy Kimmel is one of my favorite comics as he can get me to laugh, which isn't easy. I like his "fun guy-next-door personality" that I believe is similar to Johnny Carson's. I just want to pinch his cheeks, don't you? And Jimmy Fallon is such a "wild and wacky" guy. I love his "thank-you" notes.

Of course, I adore all the guys in our extended family. Why? They put up with me and give me new material to write about.

Fun Working in Atlanta

After having the $20,000 out-of-pocket expenses of kidney failure, we had to sell our adorable Palm Harbor, Florida, cottage in 1993. I had no choice but to return to Roswell, Georgia. Soon I was back working for a "for profit" college. I went into a difficult situation; the students had loved their teacher whose classes I was hired to take over. They were given no reason why she left and I took over. One large class had thirty in it with several difficult, spoiled and unhappy students. They did everything to make my life miserable. A couple of months later their teacher wanted to come back so I left.

Before I got ill in Florida, I had been working for a carpet place, making sales calls. I had taken two college classes to get my Florida teaching certification up to date. Given the choice, I would have tried harder to get a full-time teaching job or a real decorating position in Florida. All the allergy work problems I had in Atlanta didn't help me love being there after coming back. Fortunately, it wasn't long before I got a twenty-four- to thirty-hour-a-week job at a large department store about twenty miles away. I worked in the furniture department as a salesperson. Not ideal but I liked most of my co-workers. Among others, I met my very good friend Karen, who is now an artist on St. Simon's Island.

When you work on a commission basis, things can get competitive. You could leave for a quick trip to the restroom and have a sale stolen. If a guy is the only one in a family working, I can see how "the wife" could motivate you. I loved the nice discount I got. I bought new carpet for our living room and a charming blue-and-white checked sofa and loveseat for our family room. I preferred to put my money towards home furnishing and my dog shows rather than clothes.

I'm not sure how long I worked there, but I left when I should have stayed. I worked my ass off to make sales and get the sales record to keep the boss happy. Some of my sales were stolen, and I was not told that all sales needed to be specifically recorded earlier than formally instructed. It seemed like a game that our furniture manager was playing with managers of other departments. I quit, again without another job. (Don't do that.) It just seemed that I wasn't meant to be in Atlanta. I went back to doing some decorating and food demos at grocery stores plus some interesting market research.

Our youngest had left home to go into the Air Force. The oldest moved in and out for years. Although we loved each other it was not easy. Now, thanks to his wife, we have what I feel is a very loving adult relationship.

Hubby finally was thinking about retiring but wanted to sell our Roswell place first. It took over five years to do so. We started building a smaller home in Florida. Then he decided we needed a townhouse near his work in Norcross. Within six months we were moving furniture to Florida and, after the sale of our property, to our new townhouse in Norcross.

It certainly was an interesting time. I had my appendix removed and two months later had gallbladder surgery. (This was two weeks before closing on the Roswell place.) The future owner gave me one extra week to get the place all cleaned out. I had asked if I could just leave some stuff. The house was being removed from the property. The new property owner said, "No." A few days before I actually left, I met the guy who was buying the house. He said I could leave an old bed and anything else I wanted to leave.

Add to this pressure, Hubby was giving me a rough time as he was living in the new townhouse. The dogs and I stayed in Roswell so that I could clean out the house. I was stressed, tired, and thought maybe he could have been more supportive. Since I seemed to be the only one doing all the work, I was very irritated at him. Don't you know that love and hate are sometimes very close? I got over it, but at that time I was *not* happy.

What did make me happy was decorating our new digs. I

love, love, love decorating. (Look for my decorating book, *Decorating Isn't A Joke, Or Is It?,* on Amazon in six to nine months after this one comes out.)

Fun Traveling Solo

While traveling, some women always have to have a husband or friend with them. Although I wasn't traveling alone, I feel it may have been easier if I had. In 1964 I drove from Clearwater, Florida, to Dayton, Ohio, with our six-year-old and twenty-seven-month-old sons. I was primarily driving on Route 19. It was in July, with no car air-conditioning. (This was before air conditioning was common for cars and homes, and before freeways.)

The company Hubby worked for in the Clearwater area shut down their operation the last two weeks of July. I left the week before, with my oldest in the front passenger seat following the AAA TripTik maps. I was in the process of potty-training my youngest. He kept saying he wanted to "go poo." When I would stop at a rest stop, he would tinkle but was not comfortable being held on that big toilet. After nine or ten hours, we finally arrived at our destination motel in southern Atlanta and all was well after I got out his potty chair. That was it. I don't think he ever had an accident after that. It had taken forever to train our oldest son.

The next day, after a good breakfast and potty time, we headed straight through Atlanta with the windows down as the heat and truck fumes came in. On to Chattanooga toward Cincinnati and on to Dayton. Both days were long but the boys were really good—thank God! S.C. did extremely well at following our maps—a very smart six-year-old! Our youngest, T.J., napped a lot.

We arrived just before dark in Dayton at Hubby's mom's apartment. Mom was a wonderful woman who loved all of us. I believe she saw our boys much like she had with her two sons. She thought everything they did or said was cute or funny. Her other son lived in California with his family so she saw them in California; I'm not sure they came to Ohio very often. (While living in Florida or Georgia, I made the trip every year to see the relatives.)

Hubby flew in five or six days after completing his work project. After visiting Mom and my parents, who lived about thirty-five miles away, our family drove back to Florida after nice visits in cooler Ohio.

I always drove about half of our joint trips, such as our trip from Clearwater to our new home in Santa Clara, California. I was comfortable driving except for a few times I was alone and had gotten lost at twilight or after dark. No, I do not have nor do I want one of the "electronic know-it-all" things telling me what to do. Our son's electronic "damn thing" got us lost in Cologne, Germany, in an industrial area when it was getting dark.

After moving to Roswell, Georgia, I became very involved with breeding and showing our Atlantis Dalmatians. I began traveling to various Southern shows, sometimes with a girlfriend or one of our sons, but sometimes by myself. This was before I had a cell phone. I often went from Roswell, twenty-five miles above Atlanta, to stay with Dal friends in Clearwater or Sarasota, Florida. Most of these trips I did by myself. However, I wasn't as brave as a friend who went to Europe by herself.

Whatever you do, wherever you go, be true to yourself and, above all—HAVE FUN. You deserve to enjoy your life!

Fun with Florida Doctors

My son gave a friend of mine in Fort Lauderdale one of my first books, *Hold On To Your Panties And Have Fun*. The next day she called me and said, "I didn't get to your book until last evening. I fell asleep laughing. I'm wondering if I can send you a check and have you send an autographed copy of your book to my sister in Canada for her birthday."

"Of course," I said, "as long as you don't tell her anything about me. Then I want feedback since she doesn't know me, okay?"

About ten days later my friend called me back. She was down with a bad cold and could hardly talk. She said she had to call me and tell me what her sister said. The word from Canada was that it was very funny and the "perfect" bathroom book. We both laughed.

When I saw Dr. Four Eyes a short time later, I had to tell him about this. I just knew he would enjoy the story. Of course, he did. He suggested that if the book was going to stay in the bathroom, maybe it needs a plastic cover.

Sidebar: As bad as I am to him, he thanked me for being in the book. What a guy!

On another trip to see Dr. Four Eyes, he told me that he had a funny story for me. His dark eyes were full of fun as he said, "I have a much older patient, a man, whose daughter is an M.D. One day she called me and asked if I have any patients that are authors. I said I probably do. She asked me if Emily Hoover is one of my patients. When I asked why, she replied she met Emily at a book signing and figured out who Dr. Four Eyes was."

Thank goodness he thought that it was very funny. Love

that guy. However, I wasn't pleased to hear how unhappy he was with my eye pressure. He said due to my not liking eye drops to keep my glaucoma under control, I should have laser surgery again (to keep glaucoma pressure down). Oh—jolly ho. I told him I couldn't even think about it as I had to have two MRIs in the next couple of days due to my ear pain after my ear infection got cleared up. So I said, "Damn it, I guess I have to take drops again."

He grinned. He had me go to the front desk. The gal told me Dr. Four Eyes wanted to see me in a month. Damn, he didn't even have the guts to tell me himself. A few days later, after my MRI, I found out I have arthritis of the jaw. I called to schedule the laser procedure on my eyes. I'm on the waiting list as his first open appointment was in late June. I told him I would be in North Carolina. Something to look forward to—right. Can't wait for all that fun. Dr. Four Eyes told me it would be easier than when I had my cataracts removed. Cataract surgery was the easiest surgery I ever had. I can hardly wait. Yeah, sure.

The next time I see Dr. Four Eyes, I am going to really look at his face. I have noticed that in his television ads and printed material he recently sent me, he appears to have face fillers? Or perhaps a mini-lift or maybe air brushing or TV makeup??? As Abraham Lincoln said, "You can fool some of the people all of the time, and all of the people some of the time, but you can not fool all of the people all of the time." So, Dr. Four Eyes—I'm on to you. Maybe you think you look better, but hey, mister, some of us—me included—might think you had work done.

P.S. Maybe I should tell Dr. Four Eyes that his patients love him—ugly, or not. But if fillers or whatever he had done makes him feel better—go for it.

Fun with Dr. Foot Fetish

I have always had foot problems—long, thin, flat, flat feet. With pregnancy I went from an eleven AAAAA to an eleven AA, or narrow—a little easier to find shoes. Now I am an eleven-and-a-half AA or twelve depending upon the shoes. I also have arthritis in the top of both feet—the small bones radiating out from the ankle, in addition to several hammertoes. Dr. Foot Fetish came into the room. This doctor is an attractive thirty-something, blonde lady. I had heard really good things about her from her clients and from medical professionals. However, I was unprepared for what happened.

She and her top fast-typing assistant entered the examining room. Doctor takes a look and begins dictating at a very fast pace to "fast fingers," describing my feet in medical terms, mentioning my hammertoes—twice—and something about me having an intact small amount of toe hair. She had to look closer and put on her gloves and felt me up—*Very Firmly.* Three times I yelled out, "Ouch, Ouch, OUCH!!!" As she moved her hands up my legs, I felt more pain. I feel she could have found out what was causing my pain without all that *super-hard pressure.*

At this point I told her she better be careful or I'd write about her, as I gave her a copy of my first book. "What will you call me?" she asked. I said, "Probably Dr. Foot Fetish." She suggested some other name.

She got back to business asking me lots of questions. She told me she thought that my foot pain and ongoing sciatica (which is under control with exercise), plus my jaw arthritis, is caused by a pinched nerve in my back. She also asked me if I wanted to go with natural supplements or with medicine to control the pain. I'm going to try the supplements for a while. She also suggested that I limit my activities. I said, "Hell, no—

I'm going to keep on going."

She told me I will, from now on, have problems with my feet. (So, what else is new?) Let me tell you, she doesn't sugarcoat anything. She tells it like it is even if you aren't ready to hear it. She also told me I am never going to be normal or near normal again. She said, "You really do look good." (For your age, definitely implied.)

She wanted to see me in a month. I made an appointment and told her receptionist that I would expect a "book review."

I saw a photo of her children, I said I hoped they were giving her a hard time like she gives her patients. Ha, ha— don't mess with this bitch.

Hey, Doc, I would rather go to "happy hour" with you— as I do like you, but, God, you are a bit rough—some may even say tough. I am thinking that maybe I'll see you again and maybe I'll cancel.

P.S. The next day I canceled my appointment with her and made an appointment with my acupuncturist and soon felt better.

Fun with Doctor Spine and Doctor Pain

We first met after I was taken to the hospital for severe back pain.

I know I brought this problem on by trying to be forty again. Hubby had gone to North Carolina to open up the house and to put in his little garden of four tomato plants and supervise some interior painting. I just wanted to complete some spring cleaning and do a few Florida home projects. I repainted three pieces of furniture, plus washed and spray-painted our two wicker/rattan sofas. (If you don't hose wicker down every year or so, it dries out and breaks.) I had been working seven or eight hours a day trying to get the Florida house clean and tidy and getting projects finished before I was to leave.

I spent two days sitting at my sewing machine doing mending and making new valances for the North Carolina house. A friend helped me load my heavy suitcases into my new red metallic Ford Escape with turbo. (A big deal to me as I had my Ford Mercury van—red also—for fourteen years.)

The next day, as I bent over to get a cup of dry dog food out of a container in the bottom of out pantry, I felt pain. Hubby thought he should come back to Florida. I said, "I'll probably be better in a day or two." I wasn't; I was worse. I went to the doctor, seeing his assistant. An x-ray and two trips to the pain doctor and a shot, and I was still miserable!

I met Dr. Spine after being admitted from the ER in Jacksonville. He prescribed stronger pain medication and made an appointment for me in two weeks. I was still miserable. Hubby came home and was doing all the cooking and laundry. It was all I could do to live through the in-home therapy. I had to use a walker and could hardly get to the table. Sitting up was horrible unless I was in my lounge chair with a heating pad. August 8, 2016, I had kyphoplasty surgery. It was scheduled for 4 p.m., done at 8 p.m., and I was back home by 11 p.m. The home therapy eventually became outpatient therapy and then back again to Dr. Spine. By this time, I was using a cane and was on reduced pain-killers, which cut most but not all the pain.

Usually Dr. Spine's waiting room was full or nearly so. On this checkup day there was one person ahead of me. There had been cancellations due to a hurricane that was forecasted to come in about ten to twelve hours. Dr. Spine had me go from his office to the hospital around the corner for a CAT scan. When I went back to see him, he scheduled surgery for later the next week.

While in his office, I saw that he did his internship at the Cleveland Clinic. I told him my nephew did his internship there. I asked him, "Since I don't see any graduation certificates from college, could you have gone to one of those online colleges?" He thought that was really funny. His assistant held her hand to her face so Dr. Spine couldn't see her laughing. Clearly, he could hear her giggle. I told him I hope he pays her well as she is invaluable to his practice. Now she may love me. What do you think? Maybe she will remember me. The doctor recommended continuing therapy and walking. This was mid-September.

Three weeks later we were on our way to our North Carolina home. The house had been sold and we had to be out by October 28. Hubby drove up with me as I felt I couldn't manage all the driving plus Diva the Dalmatian. Diva was a very well-behaved dog but I didn't want to risk her pulling me over, nor did I feel I could deal with an overnight stay, dragging her crate in and out of my sporty SUV. Hubby insisted we drive the five hundred miles straight through. We left at about 11 a.m. and arrived at our home at 10:30 p.m. Every day, we cleaned out closets, packed up stuff for various charities, and stuffed the car for another trip to the dump.

Thank God for pain pills when I really needed them. I got off them a few weeks later. If I have back pain from housecleaning, I take CuraMed 750 mg. put out by Terry Naturally, available from my health food store.

P.S. Update: Will housecleaning kill you? I'm not sure, but through overwork I cracked another vertebrae in the fall of 2019. Heavy lifting and housework, again. I am so stupid I just kept on going with some old meds from 2016 and my last surgery. Back to Dr. Spine. After CAT scan and x-rays, I was rescheduled again for the same back surgery on January 27, 2020, to repair another disc. He wanted to get it done before it crumbled more. Surprise, surprise, surprise ... the doctor remembered me. He grinned when I asked him if he was still doing internet classes. Now I call him Dr. Internet, which he thinks is funny.

When I went back for a checkup, Dr. Spine asked me how I was doing. I said, "My lower back still hurts a lot—like I told you last fall." (The vertebra he fixed was at about the waist.) Smart-ass that I am, I said, "I guess I should have gone to Mayo." More x-rays showed the pain was caused by arthritis. Once again, I was sent to Dr. Pain. After four shots in my lower back and a few pain pills, I am better. As you age, crap happens to your body and you have to deal with it as best you can.

(It is important to remember, Ye Ol' Bitch me suggests that you keep trying to find the best doctor and get answers for yourself.) Now I will probably have to take a cane with me in case of dizziness (vertigo) or unsteadiness. And with the new ailment—I will need to wear support socks to keep from getting a stroke that could lead to more circulation problems and possible death.

Oh well, I gotta do what I gotta do. Oh, yeah—the doctor said my problems come from not enough exercise. Now I get on my sturdy exercise bike two to three times a day for fifteen to twenty minutes, and Hubby and I take a short walk, which we hope to increase in length.

As the doctor was going over my end-of-life plans, I told him not to resuscitate me. In the meantime, I am going to try to have fun as much as possible. Not as easy as it was before the coronavirus. However, this is what I am going to do in 2022. I am finishing this book and looking forward to finishing *Decorating Isn't a Joke—Or Is It?* I will have fun conversations on my phone and try to get people to laugh. I will really appreciate blue skies, light rain, green grass, the ocean breezes, seeing neighbors on walks and other friends when I am out and about. I don't get to see often. I will try to be pleasant, cheerful, and fun each and every day and will pray this damn virus leaves this earth soon, and thank God for all the good that comes our way.

Now what are you going to do?

Fun with the Carpet Guy

Recently Hubby and I noticed a couple of dark spots on our almost-new living room carpet. I asked my trusty housekeeper if she would please use our shampooer and clean it. Actually, she had noticed the spot in the fall and had shampooed it while we were up in North Carolina closing up our home there. Recently it seemed to have gotten worse. She worked on it again. It looked better—for a while. I honestly think Hubby walked in from the garage through the entry and got what I believe to be grease on it—although I did not tell him that.

Our living room is primarily his room. He listens to music and reads books or the paper in his favorite room. Keep in mind, he is semi-retired, so he spends his time between his office down the hall and here. Since he is a much tidier person than I am, this works most of the time. Sometimes we do invite people into this space. I feel he should open his mail in his office; however, Hubby does it in our living room. In order to keep our relationship in good shape, I *try* to keep my mouth shut. You save your battles for bigger things.

A week or so ago, after Hubby tried cleaning the carpet himself—without the desired results—we broke down and called in a professional. In comes a mid-thirties, neat and tidy, friendly guy. I said, "What do you think? Can you get these spots out?"

He smiled and said, "I don't know for sure; however, I will work my butt off to do so."

I said, much to his and my surprise, "Would you mind turning around?" He did without question. As he turned around, I then said, "Well, it doesn't look like you have much of a butt to work off." Thankfully he laughed.

I then asked him if he read books. He said, "Yes," so I gave him my first book. What a delight he was.

As is my habit, I asked him where he saw himself and what he saw himself doing in ten to fifteen years. When he came back the next day to do another procedure, he said, "I want to thank you for asking me what my plans are for the rest of my life. It really got me to thinking."

He went on to show me some of his art. Clearly he has talent. I suggested he might want to take more art classes as well as some classes in business. (This old bitch tries her best to encourage others.)

I *may* not be all bad.

Fun Traveling at Eighteen

Seeing the Radio City Rockettes in New York City on our high school senior trip was fun, fun, fun! What cute gals! We also saw the Empire State Building, and I was on national television on the "Today" show as I was standing outside the window, so my mother said.

Our class went by train from Washington Court House, Ohio, to Washington, D.C., where we went through the White House, some museums, the Lincoln Monument, etc. Then on to the Boardwalk and a nightclub in Atlantic City. Soon we were in New York City to stay the night and see all the sights. I remember at the nightclub having my photo taken and then buying it on a match case. None of us smoked, or didn't in front of our teacher, but this was at a time it was considered cool.

There were only seventeen in our senior class. Two of the boys had lost their dads. One had to work every day after class. The other boy had to take over all his family's farm work; he, however, graduated in my class at The Ohio State University. Other kids had part-time work. (From age seventeen, I worked on Saturdays at a shoe store.)

At this time only two or three families had a television. Everyone I knew had a "party line" phone, meaning three families shared one phone line. There were no cell phones, computers or internet. *None.*

It was a much simpler time. Harry Truman was president, after World War II was over and cars were replacing tanks in the auto plants. I can't speak for all my classmates but I believe most of them were almost as innocent as I. Kids at this time did things in groups. There were only six girls in my class. Two of the girls lived in the children's home. They were not in 4-H Club, band or any of the extra activities, and they had two or three outfits for the entire school year.

I always tried to be nice to my classmates or anyone else, but like most teenagers I was self-absorbed. I was always a joiner and competitive. I was college-bound while other girls were taking the secretarial classes. I remember several of us having fun stayover PJ parties and birthday parties. Unfortunately, I lost touch as some married right out of high school and had children soon afterwards. I *always* wanted to be a career woman! I never thought of getting married, much less being a mom. We soon had nothing in common except our high school days.

I had bonded with some of the band guys and remember playing basketball outside with some of the high school boys. I could hold my own and still love the game. I looked forward to a chance to shoot the hoops. Unfortunately, at my age now,

I wouldn't be up to chasing balls—of any kind.

Maybe some of my classmates "did it." I personally didn't know about it. I did hear from my brother that one of the cheerleaders in his class was a slut. She did flirt a lot.

If you ever watched "I Love Lucy," you would have a better idea of what life was like back then. Or maybe you saw "Leave It to Beaver." I was married about the time that came out.

I worked my way through college, graduated in 1957, and had worked for over a year before marrying my college sweetheart. If the pill had been available, I might not have married at that time. My mother put the fear of God in me about getting pregnant. "Nice girls" didn't have sex until they married.

Sixty years later he is still my sweetie—most of the time—or my old fart, but, gals, remember, he is *my* old fart. Keep your hands off, okay?

Fun with Flowers

I love, love, love to see beautiful flowers in my front flowerbeds. It puts a smile on my face and just plain makes me happy as I pull into our drive. I love most flowers but prefer those that are easy to grow. I want all the colors of the flowers to look well together. I'm not overly fond of orange flowers such as marigolds, unless used with a lot of white blooms. I really dislike orange flowers with red or blue flowers.

Some people have said women are like flowers. Really? Yes, sometimes certain girls will suddenly bloom into lovely young women. Have you heard the term "English rose" when referring to a young beauty, usually with porcelain-like skin?

Then there are women who are like narcissus. No doubt the term narcissus comes from the same root word in Latin or Greek. This is the type of woman other women may call bitch. Avoid giving your time to this type of gal because you'll never "measure up" to her standards of excellence. She is, in her own mind, always right about everything *all* the time. I know this from knowing one. She is not capable of saying, "I'm sorry." Unless you are very patient and have lots of time to devote to her, it won't end well.

A petunia type of gal is a long-term gal. She is steady, there for you, and generally is easygoing and good company. A friend to hold onto, believe me. (I am fortunate to have some like this, thank God.)

A poppy type of girl is fun, fun, fun. Watch out, she may be tiresome at times—as she can become over-obsessive and not take proper care of herself or her professional life. Her loud voice and overzealous personality could cause her heartbreak in the marketplace. She is probably the one who somehow gets by, but is seemingly always hunting for a job. This may be okay in her twenties but not at sixty. Your efforts to help her "get real" and get a job with benefits will largely go unnoticed. You can only pray for her to get her life together. I know *several* forty-to-sixty-age gals in this category. They are fun but sometimes can wear you out. P.S. All are single.

The camellia type of gal is the true churchgoer and, in her mind, never does anything wrong— *except* try to get you to be more like her. (If you want to go to heaven.) She can be a true friend as long as you don't try to educate on any other religion. She can be sweet and fun, but may have a problem having a wonderful breakfast at anyplace that might offer mimosas, or serve liquor or even wine, at any other time of day. "It smells in these kinds of restaurants," she may tell you. If one of these is your mother, you may have found yourself feeling that no matter how hard you try you can never please her. I know, as my mother was this type. For instance, as an adult in my thirties, I, with the help of my sons, worked my ass off to get "Yard of the Month." I thought she would be very pleased. When I told Mother over the phone, her response was," Oh, that's nice," as she went on to talk about her favorite topic—HER. She was a flower-cross, as most of us are with other flower types—she having huge narcissistic tendencies.

The lily of the valley type of gal is so introverted she is not interesting, even to herself. She often is one that has had a strong, perhaps abusive father and marries like kind. She doesn't do anything unless her husband either approves or tells her to do it. Poor thing is like a trampled-upon flower. She tries to come out of her shell, but often doesn't "have the guts" to follow through. You feel sorry for her; however, you have to remember every person is responsible in their life's journey. You can't help or be responsible for them, only pray for them.

The pansy type of woman is to be avoided at all costs. Like the pansy, she has two faces. She can't be trusted. She can be your very outgoing, attractive, fun club member who *appears* to be nice. One such pansy even joined a large group I belonged to in order to come to our annual Christmas potluck. (At least this is what she told me.) Although I never had any issues with her, I felt, in my gut, she was not to be trusted. Although she was married, my husband hinted that she came on to him. To my knowledge, she was the only woman to do so. She went to a dog show thing (held about two hours away) with two of her new pals. They took our mutual pal's motorhome. I soon heard, via the grapevine, she upset both gals. They left her, her dogs, bags and baggage on the street corner.

Of course, inquiring minds (me) wanted to know what

happened. So, when I ran into my motorhome gal friend, I asked her if the rumor was true. "Yes, it's true," she said. I asked, "What happened?" My friend told me that she and the other (third) gal "got into it" because the pansy had told each of them that the other had said horrible, untrue things about them, behind their backs. Apparently, the pansy gal never thought they would find out. She must have been very jealous of the others' friendship to do something like that, don't you think? Is that how to win friends and influence people? FYI: Lying will *always* get you into trouble. Although pansies can be very charming—beware!

The marigold girl is a much different sort. She loves, loves, loves money and men. Preferably good-looking men, but sometimes looks and age don't matter to her. She is a snake that usually is good-looking and probably really sexy. (At least that is what a friend and I figured out.) Right or wrong? Or she could be that a very attractive co-worker who can't live without a man. One successful businesswoman marigold I know has had one, two, three, four, five—yes, five marriages. Another friend had a relationship with a guy she "really liked." She thought he was "the one." She introduced the two. The next thing you know he is dating the "sexpot." Within a very short time he proposed to "Sexy." They soon married. The marigold even changed jobs and moved to his city with her middle-school-aged children. It didn't last long. My friend was heartbroken. Question, how could *any* decent woman do this to one of their closest childhood friends? Crazy—probably. I just hope all the bed-hopping and marriages didn't mess up her kids.

It seems money- or sex-driven marigolds don't answer to God or their family or friends. But beware, marigolds! I recently saw "this one" with her fifth. It *appears* she finally got it right this time. They seem to have a common hobby that keeps them active and busy. Good for her—him too. (I wish no ill on *anyone*.) However, I did get some real satisfaction from barely being able to recognize her after about twenty years. Girlfriend, I have to tell you, the dumped friend still looks really good. She is very attractive, while "Sexy" ain't so sexy anymore. She is three or four sizes up—not good on a short gal. And to top it off, her face is showing fat and wrinkles. Hey, what's the expression my sons use? "She looks like she was rode hard and hung up wet to dry," if you get my meaning. She looks at least fifteen years older than her friend.

Although not a real flower—be aware of *ivy*. She acts like a friend, the two of you plan things and help each other, invite each other to all your parties, etc. Then she gets very jealous and tells *big* lies. I had such a friend who told mutual friends that I had said horrible things about their show dogs. She also tried to cause problems between another "doggie" friend and me. I found out from both parties what she said. She told me that my friends had said horrible things about me and my dogs. (Don't believe what you hear.) Jealousy and envy can be poison. We don't speak. God got her good; her ugly personality has moved to her face. She never smiles. She has given up showing, which is good, as I rarely see her. I feel sorry for anyone who has no real friends. I was a very good caring friend for a long time—not anymore. Did she think I was so stupid that I wouldn't find out about her lying?

P.S. I'm smarter than I look, cookie.

Fun with Dog Names

Can you see a Saint Bernard named Godzilla? The "call name" for a female would be Zilla or for a male, Zilly.

Bulldogs would be fun to name. I thought very seriously

about getting a top-quality Bulldog show bitch named "Awesome." Yes, she was, and that *was* her name! I guess someone probably used "Rock-n-Roll" as the registered name. I have always loved the name "Rocky." I have judged Bulldogs at dog show matches and *really* appreciate good ones. However, the reason I didn't get "Awesome" is that I did my research and talked to other people who had one Bulldog. They told me that they let their dog on their sofa only for a few hours after he was bathed. This was because very soon their coats started to smell, and they have gas issues. Another person told me how heavy they were, not more than a Dalmatian, but Bulldogs can't jump up into a van and into their crate.

When I am at a dog show and see what I think is going to be a great dog, regardless of the breed, I always try to tell the owner how much I like their dog. Last fall I saw a really nice, young brindle Bulldog. He had a lovely head, topline and feet. He looked like a real winner. He was so cute with personality plus, and I think he would have been willing to go home with me. I found out this puppy won points towards his championship that day.

I have always liked a good Afghan. At a match (a fun, training show) years ago, I judged several Afghans in St. Petersburg, Florida. I gave the breed win to a nice bitch. Females are called bitches—probably because they can be. I liked the owner's silver puppy boy but felt he needed his nails trimmed, his coat wasn't as long as the bitch's, and he lacked muscle due to his age. The owner was very rude to me and told me her male should have won as she paid a lot for him after he had won a big specialty sweepstakes. Puppies can look great at six months, and then within a few months they go through their ugly stages, which I feel is what happened. A few years later, I saw a lovely silver Afghan at a dog show in

Perry, Georgia, full of confidence, his long coat groomed to perfection and moving beautifully. I believe he got a Group Three.

When the handler came out of the ring, I told him had I been judging he would have gotten the group. I asked him if the dog had gotten a Best in Show yet. He said he had gotten close, but no Best in Show. He invited me to meet the owner. Guess who the dog was—yes, the former puppy. I remembered the owner. I asked her if she remembered me judging this dog. She said no. I reminded her of my conversation and told her that had she acted that way at any AKC show, she could have all her AKC privileges taken from her. Then she thanked me for liking her dog. She *had been* rude, and she said it was a match. I told her she could tell a match judge how she thought one dog was better that day than another, but remember, these matches are done by amateurs who aren't paid, and I didn't appreciate her rudeness. Actually, I was sweet, and so was she.

Sometimes breeders and owners get "kennel blind"—meaning they think their dogs are better than others do. Most judges try to do good judging; however, some do tend to look above the head of the dog and put up a favorite handler or friend. Life isn't all about fair, is it? Sometimes, those of us who have been around awhile figure out who *not* to show to.

I would love a small bitch who I could register as Atlantis Charm On My Arm and call her "Charm." I haven't decided on a breed yet. I need to go to shows and get better educated. I have been studying Tibetan Spaniels (commonly called "Tibbies") for about twenty years. I really loved my Bichons; however, they weigh more and Tibbies don't require as much grooming. Big deal for this old lazy bitch (me).

A lot of breeders love naming puppies. Most have theme names like casts of television shows or movies, or Gold Medal winners, etc. That makes it easy to identify puppies in weekly puppy pictures. Sometimes, a dog will have three kennel names so the actual name needs to be shortened, like "Diva." Her AKC title is *Ch. Laurel* (my friend and co-breeder's kennel name) *Atlantis* (as I was the co-breeder) *Chermar's*, for Cheryl's kennel name (as Diva lived with her for a year before I got her).

Some of my favorite people think they are so cute, giving double names. The AKC name is a formal name. Most breeders try not to double-name. By double-naming, some people might call Diva "Dottie" instead of Diva.

We had a lovely puppy who got his championship under Ch. Atlantis Class Act. We and his owners called him "C.A." His sister was Ch. Atlantis Flashdance, who we called "Flash." And a brother, Ch. Atlantis Noethem's Top Spot, who was called "Tops." The fourth champion was Ch. Atlantis Bravo, who was called "Bravo." These are names that you might see in old pedigrees. When someone would mention "Flash," people would know who she was—get it?

However, people who I know and love sometimes have three different names for the same dog. Now that the breeders are getting older, they are having trouble remembering their own names. Yes, I have caught you, girlfriend, a couple of times. Maybe wine or margaritas were involved? Who knows? I won't give you her name, but she may give you her really good margarita recipe. If you have been invited to any party she throws, you may guess who she is.

I love naming puppies and I love my co-owners, who allow me to name most of our show dogs. FYI: I have *loads* of gorgeous liver names. Liver Dals are deep chocolate-brown and white, and in the past were more rare. I appreciate and have owned or co-owned some lovely livers, but out of the last five or six champions, only one is black and white.

Now I co-own a beautiful black-and-white male out of breeding with a friend living in Norfolk, Virginia. He is Ch. American Road Atlantis Harley Sportster, and his call name is Harley. Several breeder judges who saw him at the Dalmatian Club of America (DCA) Show in Ohio, Florida and St. Louis think he has potential as a special (meaning he could go Best of Show someday). What excites me is his calm yet showy personality. (Some of ours are maybe a little too much fun.) He has lovely conformation, nice spotting, and moves like a dream. He finished his championship easily. His sire is a backcross to the Pointers, which means he could help with the blockage and kidney issues some Dals inherit. Now we co-own a beautiful liver boy—a half-brother to Harley. I think Sunny could be nicer than Harley when he matures. We named him American Road Atlantis Sunset but we call him Sunny. We try to put gold, sun or red in some form in the liver Dals' name.

Why some Dal breeders breed to lines that are known to have problems is beyond me. Some breeders will breed dogs that have poor temperament. One breeder, after breeding her gorgeous male many times, finally put him down after he bit a judge. Biting is unforgivable. To some it seems it is *all* about "the winning." Showing is supposed to be about genetics and planning healthy, happy and beautiful dogs. What can I tell you? Some people seem to be just stupid.

At this point in life, regardless of my age, I love genetics and planning *healthy*, *happy* and *beautiful* dogs. What can I tell you?

P.S. What I know for sure: I truly believe that genetic problems can go back six to eight generations. If you double up on some of the big Dalmatian winners, you will likely have not only personality problems, but also could have epilepsy, copper toxication and kidney issues. I understand some breeders' stud contracts say they won't be held responsible for such. I *hate* this happening to our breed!

P.P.S. Thank you, God, for my interest in genetics and the ability to stay away from these issues 99% of the time.

Fun with Trick or Treat

Trick or treat isn't what it used to be. It was no big deal while I was growing up during the Depression and World War II. When I was three or four, I remember hobos coming to our door in southern Ohio asking for food. My mother willingly gave them peanut butter sandwiches or pie.

After my paternal grandfather's farm helpers were drafted, my daddy was asked to come home and run the farm. We moved into what had been my great-grandparents' home. My grandmother, my dad, and I all were born in this Victorian house. (Sidebar: I was born in 1935 in the middle of a snowstorm, delivered by a female doctor, quite unusual.)

This was a rough time for our country and our family. There was rationing on everything, gas, tires, shoes, clothing, sugar, meat, etc. During the war, the radio was on most of the time for all important war updates. There was no television, internet or big highways. For about five years, I had one pair of corrective shoes, ugly dog-poo brown. I remember sitting in Dad's car while they were being re-soled.

My grandfather and brother helped my dad as much as they could. At harvest time, my grandmother and mother would cook up pots of vegetables, chicken and maybe pies for all the neighboring men that helped each other with all the work.

At ten I remember I was asked to clean out the hog house with a putty knife after Daddy worked to remove most of the hardened feces. FYI: Hogs are said to be smarter than dogs; however, my Dals never slept where they pooed—just say'n.

I watched as my dad delivered a calf as well as piglets. My grandmother owned the chickens and would frequently check on them after milking her cows morning and night. I frequently hung out with her in the milking barn. At first, she milked all the cows by hand, giving a squirt of milk to a nearby cat, then leaving some in an old saucer for the rest. Later on she used milking machines, which made her life a lot easier.

At ten I was gathering the eggs and getting pecked as I did so. I helped my family weed our vegetable garden. At mealtime I set the table and then washed or dried the dishes. With a wet rag I wiped down the stairs, cleaned the bathroom, kept my room neat, and took care of my baby sister while my mother sewed or baked an occasional pie or birthday cake. My mother cooked, cleaned, made most of our clothes, washed them, hung them out on a clothesline or in the unheated wash house when the weather was bad. She soon was passing the ironing and most of the cleaning on to me, especially during harvest time when she and Grandmother canned fruits, vegetables and meats for winter meals.

Living on the farm we seldom went to the tiny local grocery store on the first floor of a small two-story home. Usually all we needed was flour, spices and sugar, if we had rationing coupons we could use. We only had sweets on our birthdays or Christmas.

I remember a friend of my dad's going into the service. He sent me a doll from the Pacific. I remember how very sad our family was when his ship sank. I recalled a classmate's family having a blue banner on their front door with four stars for their sons in the service. I also remember when three of the sons were lost and the stars became gold. I recall overhearing my mother and my aunt, who lived with us while her husband was in the service, discussing the Germans. They were afraid the Germans would come over here and rape us, whatever that meant. I remember the jubilation of World War II ending.

It was during the war that our family and I went trick-or-treating with cheap half-masks and hobo old clothes, hats covering our heads and most of our faces. Living in the country, we only went to Daddy's elderly aunt and uncles and to our grandparents. The relatives all looked surprised and pretended not to know us as they gave us a few pieces of hard candy and maybe a piece of fruit. We put them in a clean sock we carried.

Hubby, who grew up in Dayton, Ohio, just told me he didn't remember ever going out for Halloween. However, he had fun as a teenager going out the night after Halloween on a scavenger hunt and getting a lot of candy.

Fast-forward many years later when our oldest, in his twenties, asked me to make him a long caftan for a Halloween party. On the way in his old red Honda as he was getting gas, he provided a couple of cops in their cruisers a big laugh. Our six-foot-five-inch son, with his long brown hair, sandals and a belt he made out of bolts, looked like a rock 'n' roll Jesus! Halloween sure isn't what it used to be, is it?

Fun Speak'n' Southern

Often people wonder where I am from. I tell them I'm from my mother's womb. Keep in mind I am considered confused, as I was born in Ohio and lived there for eighteen years. I went to Mary Washington College in Fredericksburg, Virginia, for my first year of college. Here I was exposed to lots of Southern girls and their Southern language and their

Southern customs, language and food—yummy.

My roommate had had a big coming-out party. I had no clue what it meant to be a debutante. I found Southern girls to be very sweet and lots of fun. However, my roommate from Montgomery, Alabama, was "something else." It was the North meeting the South. I had never met someone our age who had gone to Europe. Also, I never met someone who came from divorced parents. Talk about spoiled. She would spend over an hour in the bathroom getting ready for a date when four other girls were waiting. We were housed in a private home across from the campus.

My roommate complained about my grinding my teeth while I was sleeping. She criticized my clothes and tried to educate me about bras that were more supportive and cost more. A couple of years later I upgraded to her brand. She wore fake eyelashes and lots of makeup. This girl wanted to be an actress. She was so in love with her boyfriend from high school. Maybe sending her to Europe and sending her to a girls' college was done to get her away from Bill.

I remember her saying, "Don't you think Bill is just the *cutest* boy ever?"

"No," I said, "but he seems really nice." Man, did I hurt her feelings. I really didn't mean to.

She said, "Why did you have to say that?"

"I'm sorry, I guess I'm just too honest."

I loved the Southern food, especially sausage patties, biscuits and fried apples with brown sugar. I enjoyed hanging out with several of the Virginia and South Carolina girls. I loved being in the sixty-member marching band. We wore short blue pleated skirts, matching drum-major-type hats, and off-white jackets with epaulets and brass buttons. I enjoyed playing second cornet in the dance band. We wore cute red jackets, white blouses and black skirts and shoes.

Years later after living in California and moving to Georgia, I learned a lot about the "old South." We moved to the Atlanta area in 1968. Black maids would be in white uniforms waiting for their buses. Buckhead was "the area" where the privileged lived. The area where the movies "Driving Miss Daisy" and "The Help" might have been filmed. We lived in a new neighborhood probably fifteen to twenty miles north of this area. Three years later we moved to a small farm (eight acres) farther north outside Roswell. Most people I knew did their own housework, although occasionally I got some help before the holidays. Yes, the lovely lady happened to be black. In California I had helpers from Merry Maids. They were available in Atlanta at that time.

These are some of the Southern words I have heard and their meanings:

Ailin': Sick

Ain't: Contraction of "am not"

Bad off: Really sick, likely to die

Barefoot and pregnant: Southern husband's idea of the perfect wife

Bless her heart: An expression used when seemingly feeling sorry for another—but often meaning the opposite.

Burned out: House fire

Cent: As in five cent instead of five cents

Corn likker: Corn whiskey

Country store lunch: Crackers and cheese, or can of sardines and a bottle of pop or soda

Cuttin': A piece of a plant to be put into water to sprout

Cuttin' up: Having fun

Darn: Crisscross of threads to mend a sock or garment; also, a word used by a polite Southerner instead of "damn"

Druthers: Wanting something
Ever hear tell?: "Have you ever heard?"
Every whichaways: Scattered
Favors: Looks like
Featherbed: A comforter that was filled with feathers
Fer: For
Fetch: Get for me
Fix: (has several meanings) 1. To repair; 2. To rearrange; 3. To prepare food, hair, etc.
Fix'n to: Ready to do something
Fleshed up: Gained weight (may be pregnant)
Funeral food: Food given to a dead person's folks
Georgia peach: A beautiful girl
Hard row to hoe: Hard soil or a difficult task
Haul off: 1. Items to be picked up and taken away; 2. To haul off: lose control
Head off: To keep someone from doing something (example, to head off a fight
Her'n: Hers
His'n: His
High as a pine: Drunk
Hill of beans: A worthless person or deed
Hissy-fit: A Southern melt-down
Hot enough for ya: Describing really hot weather
Hound dog: Can mean a guy who is or thinks he is sexy
In a family way: Pregnant
In the service: A domestic helper or in the armed forces
Laidly: As saved, or as crops that don't require any more hoeing before harvest
Laid up: Sick
Lasses: Molasses

Lick and a promise: A quick surface cleaning done at the last minute before company gets there

Light bread: White bread that is lighter than biscuits or dark bread

Like a pig sty: A messy or dirty house

Mater: Tomato

Mess: 1. Untidy; 2. A quantity—for instance, a mess of garden peas means enough for a meal; 3. Used to describe a fun person; 4. Messing with: used to describe someone having fun teasing another

Moonshine: Homemade corn likker or whiskey

Moving pitcher or picture show: Movie

Manase: Mayonnaise

Mustard plaster: Mustard spread out on fabric and placed on chest to sweat out a cold

Neck of the woods: Meaning that people live near each other

Neighborly: Being friendly and helpful to neighbors

No flies on her: Well groomed

Particular: As in how a lady might want something done in a special way

Pity party: A person who seems to be enjoying feeling sorry for themselves

Plum wore out: A person or item that is worn out or very tired

Puttin' up: Canning food

Raisin': 1. Used to describe raising a barn or house; 2. Raising children with good values and manners (example, "Didn't you get no raisin'?")

Rite cheer: Right here

Rite smart: A bright person

Rosen ears: Roasted corn, or cooked and ready to eat

Ruint: Ruined or destroyed

Slop: Food scraps mixed with water to feed the pigs

Sloppin': Taking a biscuit and dipping it into gravy, or a cookie into milk

Smart as a Philadelphia lawyer: Smarter than most people

Spell: As in fainting or undiagnosed illness

Spittin' image: Someone who looks like another

Spring chicken: 1. A tender young chicken; 2. Used negatively as in "She's no spring chicken anymore," describing an older lady

Sweepin' the yard: What poor folks with dirt (soil) yards did—picking up trash, then raking the dirt into patterns to look good for Sunday visitors

Tacky: 1. Doing something considered tasteless; 2. Like a *nouveau riche* person who shows off their big diamond ring, etc.; 3. Describes a girl who goes after another girl's boyfriend

Tarnation: A nebulous place (example, "Where in tarnation have you been?")

Tater: A potato

Thang: Thing

Tote: 1. To carry or take something or someone to another place; 2. A type of handbag

Takin' in washin': A person who collects someone else's laundry to wash, iron and fold for them

Tetched: A person thought to be loony

Used to could: Were able to do something in an earlier time

Waller: 1. As hogs roll in mud; 2. Someone who seemingly enjoys unfortunate crap in their life

Whitewash: Originally describing a substitute paint made of lime and water, used primarily during the War between the States; 2. Sometimes used to

describe "whitewashing" a situation—meaning to make light of the situation
Whoa!: Stop—said to a horse or person
Yawl: As in "you all" or "all of your family"
You all: As in "you all" or "all of your family"
Yawl come: You and your family are welcome.

FYI — Florida is the state where you have to go north in order to reach the "Deep South."

Fun Going to Modeling School

I'm not sure if you would consider this as solo travel, but now that I think about it, I am surprised my parents allowed it. I really wanted to go to Mary Ripple Modeling School in Columbus, Ohio—fifty miles from home. My mother didn't start driving until she was forty in 1951. On Saturdays, Mother or Daddy would drive me to and from the bus stop about twelve miles from our home. The bus had no air-conditioning. I remember the windows open and the smell of carbon dioxide.

The bus drive took, with stops, over an hour. I would arrive in Columbus dressed up in high heels with my signature model hatbox (a small, round piece of luggage). In the hatbox I believe I had my casual top, shorts and a pair of flats for exercise lessons. I had saved my money for a long time to be able to pay for the "Beginning Self-Improvement" and "Basic Modeling." I remember practicing walking with a book on my head, to help posture. (Too bad I didn't keep this up as I got older.)

Mary Ripple, who was probably in her mid-thirties, was a beautiful, curvaceous brunette, five-foot-eight and wearing a size ten. She was what today could be considered a trophy wife, as her husband was a pleasant-looking guy in his sixties—I, being eighteen, thought them an odd couple. I had never seen couples with that large an age span. They were very sweet with one another. Mary was the top model in Columbus and always featured in a multitude of the Columbus Journal's major department stores' Sunday advertisements. I was just an innocent country girl who wanted to become more sophisticated. I was hoping to go into television as a talk show hostess. I did everything Mary told me to do.

At that time, I was five feet nine and a half inches tall, not bad-looking but not super slender. I was told to exercise in order to reduce my hips. I did my exercises and tried to lose the "fat butt." Mary, I believe with Mr. Ripple's help, had put together an outline of classes that taught us about wearing only solid colors, no prints. She taught us how to wear scarves, our best colors, how to walk like a model (putting the ball of the foot down before our heel), how to gracefully remove a coat without it touching the floor, and how to get into and out of a chair and a car without looking awkward. She also taught us some manners, or tried to in my case. My mother felt it was good for me as I had grown so fast and loved playing basketball and hanging out with my guy buddies and was a bit of a tomboy.

My Aunt Emily and my mother were very fashionable when they made the effort. I remember my mother looking so beautiful in a fur-collared camel wool wrap coat and a fashionable felt hat. She was beautiful before she got so ill when my sister was born. This while my dad had his good government job as a supervisor of a Civilian Conservation Corps (CCC) camp. My mother had made friends with a couple who owned a very nice dress shop so I believe she got a discount.

When Dad left that job and moved us to his parents' farm (to help work the farm after Grandfather's workers left to go into the World War II Army). Farming is a very hard way to make a living. After the war and Grandfather's death, Grandmother wanted us to move out so her favorite younger son could take over the farm. (Later, due to poor management and a downward trend in farming, there was never any inheritance left for my dad.) With the increased expense of buying the farm, things did not get much better, even though Daddy was back working for the government as a county conservation agent. With his degree in agricultural engineering, he had the background to advise farmers on improving their soil drainage and crop rotation. He and my brother ran our new farm. Unfortunately, it fell mostly on Larry as Daddy was only home on the weekends.

When she was young, my grandmother, who was a seamstress, taught my mother how to sew. My mother taught me and I taught my sister. Except for underwear, we girls made almost all our clothes. When I was seventeen, as a 4-H project, I made a "complete outfit." This included a white wool dress with four big black buttons on the wrap top. To complete the outfit, I made a slip, bra, panties, and a black, faux Russian lamb wool, three-quarter-length wrap coat. Mary Ripple loved the sophisticated look. Even today this outfit would be considered chic. I was happy I won a blue ribbon.

Through self-improvement and modeling classes, I became aware of fashion design and learned what looked best on me. This was helpful as I was so tall and, yes, awkward. I learned about hair styling, makeup and clothes. These classes helped me have confidence and begin a sense of style. At that time, I was tall and had a thirty-six, twenty-six, thirty-six figure. Nice proportions maybe but not reed-thin, like model types. I have never thought of myself as good-looking, but looking back at old photos, at least I wasn't downright ugly. After I reached thirty, it has been a constant battle to keep my weight down. Showing my Dalmatians helped for thirty years. Then I asked a friend if my age and twenty-plus pounds were keeping my very nice dog from winning. She, being honest, confirmed this. At that time, I started having a co-owner or handler show our dogs.

FYI—If you are like me at about twenty pounds overweight, we are considered obese. I need to watch size portions and limit carbohydrates and desserts. At one point I was borderline diabetic. After taking inexpensive cinnamon pills and dropping ten pounds, I am now in the normal range.

FYI 2—After reading about intermittent fasting and learning about "when" to eat, not what, I have lost about forty pounds in the last two years. I eat two to three meals daily, but go from 8 at night to 10 or 11 a.m. before eating again. I try to eat moderate-size meals to eat healthy. I weigh myself every morning. I still have a glass of wine and sometimes dessert. This is the ONLY diet that I have found works for me long-term.

Fun with Fashionistas

Some, if not most, fashion trends are said to start with the young gals who visit thrift stores. They take old clothing and make a few changes and, ooh-la-la, a new trend begins. Soon a famous actress is wearing the "new look." There are some gals who jump on the bandwagon and are called "early adapters." As time goes on, the next group is called "late adapters." After that, you see similar styles being mass-produced. When the trend becomes commonplace, the trendsetters move on to new styles. I guess this could be called a circle of fashion.

My style has been referred to as "my branding" by other authors. This is because I dress to go with my book covers. When I did a book signing for my first book, which has a red cover with white and black accents, I would wear either black or white pants, a red or black top, and a jacket in black or red. My book tablecloths consist of a solid red one that drapes to the floor, topped by a smaller black square one with white polka dots. Having taught advertising and fashion classes, I came up with this look to tie in with "my book," and for signings, I always wear some version of red and black. People comment on "my look." I have even been called a fashionista. I've been called a lot worse, too. (For instance, "Big Ass," by my brother.)

I got to thinking about my style. I tend to wear a lot of black and white with splashes of color. I wear pants ninety-nine percent of the time as they are more comfortable to me than skirts or dresses. I have a few long skirts, which I seldom wear. I love, love, love jackets. If it is too hot for a jacket, I wear a long-sleeved top, and sometimes with a fashionable lightweight vest. I have several quilted ones and three or four long draped ones. These looks, with a pair of hoop earrings, are my standard "going out" looks. For more formal dinner-dance type things, I have some elegant travel pants in both black and white and several longer dressy tops. Sometimes I will wear a statement type necklace—always with hoop earrings. Or I might add a zebra, leopard or vividly colored scarf.

I used to have a few people who, when I was dressed up, would say I looked pretty. (Always a surprise to me.) When I started wearing big glasses, I would get compliments on my "neat glasses" and I still do. I often get positive comments on how good I look ... for my age, I'm thinking. I tell people, "I hate to tell you this, but I think your vision is going."

Everyone should find their own style. I found I like simple classic lines. What I try to do is update my look each year with a few new pieces and accessories. Because I am tall, I can get by with wild, colorful print tops or a long black-and-white zebra knit skirt with a longer black top. I seldom buy fad fashions. I don't like to see teenage clothes designed for thin girls on heavier or older gals. Do you? For instance, leggings with a short top that shows their big ass, or a short dress that does the same thing when they bend over. Think about the "picture" you make coming as well as going or bending over, okay?

When I am home cleaning, I wear jeans or tan pants and a longer shirt-type top. I make an effort to put on makeup and look decent. I am comfortable, yet if I have to run to the grocery store I don't have to change clothes. Why? I do this for myself and for Hubby, who shaves every day. I have to admit that sometimes I write, do laundry, and watch Hoda and Jenna and/or Kelly and Ryan in my PJs. Changing clothes is not something I want to do. When buying new clothes, I bring them home to try on or get them from a shopping channel.

I have friends who "really like" to buy new clothes for any event. I usually don't, as I must confess that due to over-buying in the past and keeping clothes a long time, I really don't need new stuff. In the past, I have always used older clothes for everyday. Now I feel the need to wear clothes that give me a lift, so recently I bought a couple of new long shirts for everyday. Maybe it is because I'm not dressing up for book signings two or three days a week like I used to.

Do you watch "Project Runway" or "Project Runway Junior"? You can learn a lot about fashion, girlfriend. These shows could be the start of your becoming a true "fashionista." Regardless, each person needs to find their own style. For those of you who are late teens or early twenties and not so sure of what really looks good on you, have patience. Go to an upscale store and ask a fashionable saleswoman to help you to select a few basic pieces. Tell her you need her advice within *your* budget. *Don't* let her or anyone talk you into going over your budget. It might be good to take a thrifty, older, fashionable friend or your mom with you. Keep your receipts so you can return any items that you may decide aren't for you or are over budget. (Make sure you can return items and know the time limit.)

Other suggestions: Go sightseeing—meaning, go to an upscale shopping center and walk around taking photos of outfits you like. Then get a fashion-forward older friend's advice on what would look good on you. Do not try to copy a friend's look or a current trend. *You need clothes that make you feel good as well as look good on you.*

Another suggestion is to "get your colors" done. This could be a fun, friends get-together. You try on various tops or hold various colors of fabric next to your face and have your girlfriends tell you what colors are best on you. Listen to people when several friends say something looks good on you. Some people have warm complexions and look better in cool colors. Warm complexions are those that are more pink, usually blushing more easily. These gals look good in pink and coral, but red is *not* their color. It makes the skin look too pink. If you are a "warm" and *love* red, wear red skirts or pants paired up with, say, a navy or black top.

In my heart I am still a bit of a slob. Maybe what changed me was moving to a small town where I usually go out more often and run into people I know. And, to be honest, being an author, I expect more out of myself.

P.S. Okay, now that I have either put my slob clothes in the trash or passed them on to charity—I am either a bad person, or a reformed slob.

Fashion Glossary

- **Fad:** A new look that goes out of fashion just as quickly as it came in.
- **Fashion:** Prevailing styles at any given time.
- **Fashion trend:** Direction of styles at the time, going towards a future look.
- **High fashion:** New costly fashion that has become acceptable by some fashion experts and costs thousands of dollars.
- **Silhouette:** The outline of a garment or person.
- **Style:** This is an expression used to describe unique features of the cut or design of an article of clothing.
- **Fashion customs:** Established usage and socially approved.
- **Status:** Standing or rank of a designer or the overall place of a designer's work.

Fun at Party Time

My favorite entertaining is a covered dish event. We had several of these for the Kennesaw Kennel Club while living in Roswell, Georgia. The club provided a big ham and the members were asked to bring two items. They could choose hors d'oeuvres, salad, main dish, side dish or dessert. No one had to sign up; they just brought two items and it worked out great. The secret is two items per couple. We always had lots of food and fun.

These parties were held at our home, where we had a

large living room, extended by former owners to twenty-six by twenty-six feet, and a middle room I used as a dining room. We had a *very* small kitchen with a forty-two-inch round table where we placed the hors d'oeuvres and desserts. The rest of the food was on the dining room table. With borrowed folding chairs and tables, we were able to seat fifty people. This was because, besides the big living room, we had a seventeen-by-twenty-foot Florida room that the former owner had added to this 1940s house.

My most recent "covered dish" party was a couple of years ago with girlfriends from our former TOPS group (Take Off Pounds Sensibly). We jointly agreed to have everyone bring a salad with me furnishing the drinks, tea, colas or wine. Afterwards the fifteen of us watched a chick flick. It was a lot of fun, my guests said.

Among the *big* parties I've planned was Hubby's and my fiftieth anniversary indoor picnic. It was on the Fourth of July weekend in Franklin, North Carolina, at a rustic country club near our small summer cottage we had for thirteen years. About one hundred guests were invited to a barbecue buffet. Each guest was given drink tickets. If someone wanted to drink more, they paid for them. I did this for two reasons: one, I didn't want to be responsible for any traffic accidents in this curvy mountain area; two, to keep the costs down. We had a disc jockey who played our favorites. Two of my friends provided music; one played the flute, the other sang. We were thrilled that several of our college friends and my roommates came, my Dalmatian friends, plus longtime friends and locals I knew.

Because it was a long weekend, I planned no-host restaurant meals plus a visit to Highlands, North Carolina. Some of the friends and family went hiking with Hubby. I also planned a goodbye evening meal for about twenty relatives and out-of-state friends. For guests to sit and eat, I bought a couple of six-foot-long folding tables and used the two round porch tables we had. Our dining room table and buffet held the simple food I served. Guests made their own sandwiches. In addition, there was cole slaw, a relish tray, fresh tomatoes, baked beans and brownies. My boys helped get it all together. This party provided us with lots of wonderful memories.

The second big party was my eightieth birthday party held at a nearby Florida restaurant. It was another one hundred people. My favorite memories are the fun I had with family and getting to dance with a couple of my buddies. One of them was the husband of my deceased best friend Cheryl, Buddy, who's like a super brother to me. (I talk to him every few weeks.) There were some of my Dalmatian buddies, newcomers and author friends.

It was wonderful to hang out with out-of-town relatives and good friends. However, one of my author friends really embarrassed my family and me by doing a long—what she thought was a funny—monologue. She had asked me if she could do a roast for me. Stupid me, I said yes. I thought it would be funny but it was not. She, without wine, is normally a sweet, lots of fun, polite Southern gal. What she did was tasteless—not a roast. I'll give her credit as she called (one of the few) to thank me for inviting her to my party, telling me she had a really good time. I said Hubby was upset with her monologue. She said she was sorry—and I forgave her, especially when a beautiful basket of fruit and a sweet note arrived within an hour of our conversation.

Another negative was just how much everyone drank— from 2 to 4:30 p.m. One guy broke two full glasses of wine and a couple of gals, the owner told me, drank enough for several guys. The bar bill alone was $1,200. Unfortunately, way, way, way over budget. I love big parties but if I have any more parties at a restaurant or resort, it will be a smaller two-drink ticket event, or in all probability just family. Guess what people won't be invited? I would love a cruise with family, or maybe just a girlfriend luncheon. Sometimes you don't really know people until they drink too much. My advice, go with two tickets.

In the fall of 2019, Leslie and I gave a bridal going-away party for Carlie, "Air Force Annie" (whose story appeared in my first book). I asked her friends to bring finger foods or a salad for a Sunday afternoon get-together. We provided iced tea and soft drinks, and the gals were told they could bring wine if they wanted. (I did not want to be responsible for them driving 30 to 40 miles drunk.) We also provided an assortment of cupcakes.

The invitation also asked them to bring a wrapped old paperback for a "Bad-Ass Book Exchange." The invite said the party was 1:30 to 3:30 p.m., but apparently the twelve gals were having so much fun they didn't leave until almost 6 o'clock. We had fun getting to know each other and playing a couple of games Leslie found on the internet. Another game the party honoree and I came up with was "20 Questions—Who Knows Carlie Best?" I gave the winner one of my books. The gals enjoyed each other so much they want to have a meal together once a month. Sounds like a lot of fun to me. Most of them were in Carlie's age range—40s. Maybe Carlie will drive up from Tampa for a weekend so she can join us.

P.S. Remember, I told you, you should hang out with people younger than you, because as you get older, you lose more and more of your old friends.

P.P.S. In 2020, I lost twelve people I knew—several I had met when I was in my twenties and thirties.

Fun with the Mystery Man

Hubby is now eighty-eight. I met him when he was twenty-three. We married when he was twenty-six. Even though we have been married over sixty years, I still don't understand him. He is known to be a kind, sweet guy. But frankly I often find him a "mystery."

We are not the kind of couple who always need or want to hang out together every spare minute. We love and trust each other.

When I met him on a blind date, I thought he had a cute grin and mischievous hazel eyes. I soon found him to be a super-bright mystery man. He wasn't and isn't a big talker but is more the strong silent type. Sometimes he says profound things that really shock me, like, "You're right." In sixty years, he has *maybe* said it six times, and I almost faint. Are you getting my drift here? Because he and I both know he is smarter than I, he thinks he is *always right* about *all* things. And, damn it, he usually is!

But sometimes I do know more about certain things than he ever will. For instance, what herbs and vitamins could help him. Will he consider my advice? Hell, no! Another example is interior design. He knows zip, but that's not what he thinks. I tell him he can tell me what he likes and dislikes personally but not what is the best in design. If he tries—and he *will*—to continue telling me what looks good, I finally tell him I'm the one who has studied design. I have read countless books and have taught it at the college level. I remind him that I don't tell him what to do concerning microwaves and space stuff. By this time, my voice will have risen to the point I scare myself. It is a mystery to me how a very bright engineer who never took an art or design class can think of himself as an expert. I just don't get his reasoning.

Another example of weird thinking, in my humble opinion, is the idea of asking me out to breakfast. Of course, it isn't often that I am up. He has no idea of where he plans to eat. This is how it goes. While some men golf, some go to bars, some hang out with their buddies, my Hubby's "big deal" is to go out to breakfast usually alone. But guess what? He never knows where he is going until he gets up to the traffic light. Question, does his car decide? (Stay with me.)

Hubby will say, "Oh, you're up and dressed. Do you want to go out to breakfast?"

"Where are you going?"

"I don't know, where do you want to go?"

"I don't know [as I don't often go]—what do you suggest?"

Then he will mention one or two of his favorite places. We decide. You need to understand he goes to about five different restaurants. He has a place where he gets blueberry pancakes, another has peanut butter pancakes, etc. Our relatives all want to know where he is going before going out with him too.

Another artsy-fartsy thing—sort of—is his lack of fashion sense. On occasion, he will tell me I look nice. How he knows this I have no clue, as he is not a fashion person. He is, after all, an engineer. When we are going out, I sometimes ask him to change his clothes. He has never cared what he wears, and as a result he has committed a few out-and-out *horrible* fashion no-no's!

When we moved to Atlanta and I was teaching, I had to leave for work before Hubby. Of course I got home before he did. This was the wild, hippie-inspired sixties, okay? He had on a purple shirt with a tan, brown and gray diagonal striped tie, and, to top it off, his pants were a small check, made up of red, navy and white. Unbelievable, right? The pants soon found their way to the bottom of a charity bag.

In many ways my Hubby is a simple guy. He loved his work. After we moved to Atlanta and he went to work at a new company (with friends from Clearwater), his hours completely changed. He left home at about seven-forty every morning and came home about five-thirty for dinner, prepared by ye ol' me. By six-fifteen he left for evening hours, coming home about nine to nine-thirty. He was home Friday evenings. Saturdays he would leave home about nine to nine-thirty a.m. and be back home by two p.m. This was his normal schedule.

He and the boys went with me to some of the dog show practice classes and some of the actual shows. I, along with the other wives, understood the importance of getting the company off, running and profitable. Within a short time, I was told Hubby's inventions were instrumental in the company's achievements and success. However, this schedule went on for almost twenty years.

Finally, when Hubby got our sons into Boy Scouts, he would take time out for weekends and summer camp. During the summer I would take our boys to Ohio to spend time with our relatives for about ten days, hitting a couple of dog shows. Hubby preferred to stay in Georgia and work. However, our family was able to go to the D.C.A. show in northern California. We had a nice visit with Hubby's mom and his only brother and his family.

The Mystery Man, some have said, has become "a loner"—or maybe he always was one. Since I am a "people person," I don't quite understand how he can visit and be friendly with family, and then—I guess after thirty to forty minutes with us—he retreats to the living room and his reading stash. Maybe hearing aids distort sound too much?

To me, he is THE Mystery Man.

As I do a flashback on our lives together, I remember giving him a couple of birthday parties. In fact, I gave his first one when he turned twenty-eight. I'm sure his mom, a loving working widow, had a cake-and-ice-cream meal for him when he was a child but never did a big party, as his birthday is on December 18. When we were growing up, people usually did not make a big deal out of birthdays. I surprised him with a party that was made up of people he worked with and their spouses. We had cake, ice cream, beer and wine, lasting about two and a half hours. He was surprised and pleased. His second was at forty, in Roswell, Georgia. This one was larger, consisting of work people and our Dalmatian friends.

The last one was when he turned sixty, consisting of mostly the same people. We had simple food, tea, wine and beer. The Mystery Man informed me after his sixtieth that he didn't want any more parties. So, I respected his wishes. I have a hard time with anyone turning down a party, if you get my drift. In between those birthdays, and since the last one, we go out to eat, sometimes with family if they come to visit.

But, hey, we do have some fun together, as after all we do have two sons. I remember a couple of fun happenings we had at airports. The first was in Atlanta after I came home from a European trip I had taken with our twenty-something-year-old grandson. From a distance of about forty feet, Hubby and I held out our arms, for an embrace, as we ran towards each other. It was fun and funny to us. I think we had seen it in a movie. The next one happened in Jacksonville when a cool older guy was playing jazz music in the large open area before one got to the baggage claim. We danced as onlookers grinned. Piano player told us that doesn't happen often as most people are in a hurry.

FYI—Sometimes it is good to take a few minutes to put

some joy into your life and others. Always remember that the best gifts you can give to others and yourself are fun and happy memories, Give a smile, get a smile. Give a hug, get a hug. Get a laugh and, man, you will feel great. At least that works for me.

Mystery Man has always had a problem spending money. We both grew up during difficult times of the Depression and World War II, when our families struggled to have good food on the table. We had food but sometimes we had a lot of bread or potato type dishes with very little meat. I hate bread pudding because that was about the only dessert we had during World War II, unless Mother saved up on her food stamps for birthdays or holidays. During the war everyone had rationing stamps. Our nation's first priority was feeding the troops. Not fun! We had rationing of some foods (meat and sugar, for instance), clothes, shoes, automobile tires and gasoline. I believe even coal we used to heat our homes was rationed. Keep in mind *no* television, internet or modern conveniences like dishwashers or air-conditioning. Yet, we managed to have family fun playing cards or board games. We also had community events and church—that was it.

I need to tell you my Mystery Man is a nicer, sweeter, kinder person than his "bitch" wife. Oh, yes, you probably figured this out long ago. However, Mystery Man can and does still surprise me, as you will find out in the car chapters. Do you have a fun mystery man? Here's hoping.

Fun Getting Lost

My family has suggested that maybe they should give me a GPS. Maybe they should but I do not want one, kiddo. Why? Because I have interesting adventures I wouldn't have if I didn't get lost.

One time years ago, I was following a friend to his house to look at an antique he wanted to put into my Roswell, Georgia, shop, The Strawberry Unicorn (Decorating and Antiques). We came to a busy four-way stop. He was in a green van. Apparently, he turned right. While I was waiting for my turn, another green van in front of me turned left. So what did I do? I followed him. The next thing I knew, he was turning into a drive. I followed and parked next to him. When the guy got out, it was *not* my friend! Embarrassing? Yes!

To make matters worse, his wife was outside giving me "the look." "Lady, why are you following my husband?"

I rolled down my window and said, "I guess I followed the wrong van." Fortunately, I retraced my route and found my amazed friend sitting close to the stop sign. Perhaps I should have STUPID engraved on my forehead.

The reason I don't want a GPS is that when in Europe near Cologne, Germany, with our youngest, the GPS got us really lost! Again, it wasn't in the best of areas. Even though our son speaks some German, he didn't want to stop and ask directions. What man does? If I have gas and it is daylight, I don't mind getting lost—but not at night or when the sun is going down. I get *very* anxious!

Recently, I stayed north of Atlanta with a friend. I was about two hours from our North Carolina home. Amazingly the trip home took almost five hours, as I missed the turn to Route 52 from Highway 400 over to Gainesville and 441. Years before, I had taken Tex, our handsome Dalmatian, over to a handler who lives near where I turned. As I was going around and up mountains, I stopped for directions—I must have turned left instead of right and ended up going up another mountain from two lanes to one, to a dirt road with lovely homes. I passed seven beautiful wineries in north

Georgia. At one point I may have been close to Tennessee. Finally seeing a car parked in front of a home, I rang the doorbell. A very nice middle-aged lady gave me directions. I gave her a bookmark. Ha, ha, ha. Then, taking her directions, I was on the right road and ended up finally going east. With my lack of a directional brain, anything is possible.

Once again, I got lost going to a dog show in Greenville, South Carolina. Fortunately, I got back on track with just one stop. However, when one of my Dal friends and I were to meet friends at a Dal dinner party, we got *super* lost. My friend's phone had been down so we stopped to ask directions about four times. Added to that, we turned around at least ten times. We finally gave up. When we went around the same cemetery *several* times, I was feeling that maybe God was calling me to live there. It started to get dark, which made me very anxious, as we were in an industrial area. This is funny now, but wasn't at the time.

I will say Greenville is a very attractive city with lots of tree-lined streets and good restaurants. The people are just so darn sweet! They will let you in when you need to change lanes and they are so nice when you ask directions. Apparently, they never lived in Atlanta or south Florida where drivers dare you to move over.

Don't I have an interesting life? Even though I love Greenville and have gone to dog shows there for nearly fifty years, I still get lost. This party girl really hates to miss a party—believe me. Fun friends, a good dinner and a glass or two of wine—who could ask for more?

P.S. Well, maybe *if* I come back to earth in another life, God, I would really like a better brain.

Fun Being Beautiful

"To be beautiful is the birthright of every woman," said Elizabeth Arden. She was the founder of Elizabeth Arden makeup. (I use her cream foundation and cream.) People often tell me I have lovely skin, (for my age is implied.) No— I am *NOT* beautiful, but I try every day to put my face on. When I go out, I try to look my best because you never know who you may run into. In my case, I live in a small community and often run into people I know. But beautiful, I certainly *do not think* so. However, *years ago* my Hubby said I was beautiful. (You know what he wanted.) What is really surprising is I have had women at book signings say I am beautiful. I say, "Sorry, but your eyesight is going." I am not used to compliments. (Maybe because I was never good enough for my mother.)

On the other hand, I have a friend, nearly my age, who begins her day with frumpy morning hair, looks herself in the mirror and says, "Hi, Gorgeous." That's how she starts her day with a laugh. What a fun lady!

Recently I overheard a conversation between a hairstylist and a client, as we were sitting next to each other getting our hair shampooed. This lady told her stylist that she hadn't worn makeup in thirty years. She said if people didn't like the way she looked they didn't have to look at her. I wondered why she was getting her hair colored.

Research shows that people respond better, the more attractive the other person is. If you don't try to look your best, doesn't that show a lack of self-respect? Wouldn't your appearance affect your ability to progress in your job or in your life? The American Cancer Association passes on this statement: "Look good—feel good." I believe that's true.

If you are really lazy or lack funds, what about using a tinted moisturizer? That will help your skin feel good and slow the wrinkles and would only take a few minutes to put on. A little mascara and lipstick and off you go.

Face your face, and do something to make your hair look better. Makeup and hair styling are as important as what you are wearing. If you are single and looking, it is very important to always look your best. Guys like gals that are well groomed and attractive. That means taking showers, eating right, and exercising to stay at or get to your best weight. It also means taking care of your skin and hair and using at least a little makeup. The better looking you feel, the more confident you will be.

Let's talk about clothing for a minute. (I taught fashion classes at the college level.) If you want to always look good but have limited funds or want to save the planet, go for a basic color like black, brown or navy. Add scarfs and tops in color to give your outfits and your spirit a lift. I wear a lot of black and white with pops of color. I like and feel best in brighter colors like red, hot pink, bright yellow, turquoise and kelly green. However, at home I usually wear blue jeans and a chambray shirt or often an older knit shirt.

In winter when I go out, I usually wear black pants and a colorful top, and a black-and-white jacket or maybe black pants, a black dressy tee and a bright jacket or a colorful vest. In summer I usually wear white pants and a bright top and matching sandals. To me this makes life easy. I always have something that looks nice. I love fashion and am aware of fashion trends but I am not a slave to fashion. No matter how old my things are, I usually get a compliment on how nice I look. I buy clothes that cover "the bumps." Maybe you know what I mean.

I have two longer skirts I sometimes wear in the winter with black or red boots. The boots are fake-fur-lined. I get teased about them, as rarely do I need "the fur" in Florida. I like long pants that are ankle length or longer, and a bit wider from the knee down. Why? So my long feet are not as prominent. I seldom wear my ankle-length knit skirts. They look good with longer tops as I am tall, but, frankly, I feel more comfortable in pants. I am sharing this information on what I wear as perhaps my secrets might help you.

I feel there are a lot of good fashion magazines today that we can all learn from. Study the basics and beware of getting caught up in the model bodies or in fashion fads that are temporary. Look for trends (not runway-crazy creative looks).

For those on a budget, look for end-of-season sales or consider top quality at your local consignment shops. You probably need to invest in a good winter coat, a couple of pairs of good pants and or skirts, good shoes and a nice handbag or two. You can spend less on tops and maybe replace them more often.

Gals that like dresses—I suggest you go for basic solid colors in addition to colorful vests or jackets. These should be of good quality. You can add colorful scarves from your local discount stores.

A word about skirts and dresses. My daughter-in-law always looks great! It helps that she is downright beautiful. She takes the time to do her hair and makeup perfectly. She loves fuller skirts that hit lower calf. Sometimes she wears dresses of the same length. She coordinates her earrings and necklaces. With the beginning of knee and foot problems, she wears stylish but comfortable shoes and boots. She always carries a big bag. If she doesn't pare down the items in her purse, I predict—back problems. She is not model-thin, but always looks *marvelous*!

P.S. If you wear skirts or dresses, please wear panties. And for heaven's sake, please wear nude underwear under white, okay?

P.P.S. Question: Are people who don't wear makeup maybe cutting back on laundry or deodorant? Just asking.

Fun Moving Through the Years

Most of the time moving is hectic, hectic, hectic, right? This is very difficult for people like me, who have a hard time making decisions. Do I keep it, pass on to family, sell or give to charity? Maybe I can use it?

If it is to be a local move, it is much easier as you probably will do most of it yourself. When considering long distance moves, you really *need* to check out at least three moving companies. Look for recommendations from others. If you have heavy items like a baby grand or a large glass table, you will be paying *lots* more. Sometimes it costs more to move furniture across country than it does to replace. Unless you are really attached to pieces, you should consider replacement. Most cities and even small towns have resale shops that are always fun to explore.

Hubby and I have lived in three rentals, an apartment in West Hartford, Connecticut, a rental house in St. Petersburg, Florida, and another in Largo. When our oldest was about eighteen months old, we bought our first three-bedroom, two-bath, two-car garage home in Clearwater, Florida.

During the time we owned the Clearwater house, I taught junior high one year and had another son. I decorated model homes, one for The Better Homes and Gardens Parade of

Homes, and taught adult interior design classes. These were classes I developed for the Pinellas County School System adult program. I became vice president (program chairwoman) of a large group of the American Association of University Women (AAUW) in Clearwater. (This organization was formed in the 1800s to allow women to continue learning after college.) We had all kinds of study groups, including a book reviews group, community events history, etc. (I was in AAUW in California, Georgia and Florida, before becoming president of the Roswell, Georgia, branch.)

About seven years later, Hubby changed jobs and moved us into a townhouse in Santa Clara, near San Jose in northern California. I taught high school economics, including classes in interior design, sewing and childcare. At this time, I was enrolled in graduate classes from the University of California, as well as San Jose State and later San Francisco State. I also developed a program for high school students who were interested in working in the childcare field. I supervised them while they interned in the local day care center. At the same time, I was active in the local Junior Woman's Club and on the board of missions for our local Methodist church. Hubby and I also were in a young couples' church social group. I was caring for our two growing sons, a home with lots of do-it-yourself home projects. How did I manage all that? I was young, that's how!

Our first California home was a three-bedroom, two-and-one-half-bath townhouse with a carport in Santa Clara. Two years later after selling our Florida home, we were able to sell the townhouse and bought a lovely three-bedroom home in a former apricot orchard in Los Altos. It had two and one-half bathrooms and a two-car garage. We purchased it in 1965 for about $37,500. We worked very hard at cleaning and redecorating.

This home, probably my favorite, was a charming clapboard ranch with a front Dutch door. You might have seen this kind of door in old movies. California doesn't seem to have flying bugs, so if you wanted fresh air, you opened the top and could keep the bottom locked. It was and probably still is a safe community. In 1968 we sold it fast at about $41,500. The people who bought it made *no* changes, then sold it for—get this—$1.5 million in about 2000. The area is now "out-of-sight pricey," as it is part of the Silicon Valley. We looked it up on Zillow and, with major changes, five years ago it was worth $4.5 million. Now, who knows.

When the boys were in second and fifth grades. we moved to Georgia. Hubby was invited to join a new company with former co-workers from Sperry Microwave. He was now employed by Electromagnetic Science in Atlanta. I've been told Hubby was instrumental in their worldwide success. He continued to work part-time for Honeywell, who bought out the company a few years ago. Apparently, he was amazing at coming up with new designs in microwaves, satellites, and ferrites (whatever they are). He got paid a salary, not much extra for patents. (He has over twenty.) He is a brain, what can I tell you? So are our sons and grandson. It ain't easy being me, surrounded by men who are a *lot* smarter. However, I hold my own verbally.

When we moved to Georgia, we bought a house in Tucker (northeast of Atlanta.) Three years later we moved to a much older, larger home with eight acres in Roswell, northwest of Atlanta. We owned this property for nearly forty years. *Buyer beware!* ALWAYS get a home inspection before closing on any property, and have an attorney help with all closings. We barely qualified for this home purchase with my teacher's pay and Hubby's income. What we didn't count on were multiple heating problems and much bigger operating expenses and taxes. After I received an excellent teacher review, I, along with two other very good teachers, was let go. I worked numerous part-time jobs until I got back into decorating, hired by Davison's, Atlanta's premier department store.

In 1985 I had an ovarian cancer tumor removed, grade one. No after-treatment was recommended. A month later I was referred to a lovely woman M.D. who believed in vitamins and herbal therapy. The start of my obsession with supplements. Hey, at eighty-plus and I'm still here and still writing books, walking and talking, probably too much.

Unfortunately, Atlanta did not agree with me physically, as a day without a sinus headache was a *very* blessed day. I continued to take allergy shots and gave up foods I was allergic to—mainly white bread, milk, cheese, tomatoes, fish, pizza, mac 'n' cheese, spaghetti, tomato soup, grilled cheese sandwiches, and peas. In addition, I found out I was also allergic—get this—to tissues! Talk about life-changing.

However, about ten years later I was able to start adding most of the foods back into my diet. Recently I have had several bad food allergy rashes, yet blood tests showed nothing so I am keeping a food diary. I know I can't eat strawberries, peanuts, most cheeses, fish, melon, etc. When I go to some restaurants, I have *very* few choices, especially in Italian ones. (Question, why can't Italian restaurants serve more interesting salads?)

Hubby finally realized just how miserable I was in the Atlanta climate. (I lived all year for May, June and July.) After I recovered from cancer, we bought a small Cape Cod style cottage with three bedrooms, two baths, and a one-car garage in Palm Harbor, Florida. This was a place I could escape to when I was miserable. It was fun to decorate.

Earlier, in the mid-seventies, we'd had a small mobile

home in a very nice park in Clearwater. (Lovely mobile home parks with clubhouses are quite common in Florida.) I worked in the decorating business for a dear friend of mine. Two years later, I moved on to a large furniture store where I made more money. When a person works on a base salary plus commission, it isn't easy. I was able to work with top furniture lines, good workrooms and lots of neat clients. I also taught college-level interior design classes. Hubby and I took turns driving to see each other.

My career always was more interesting in Florida, or maybe I just had more interesting clients, and of course I was a different person when I felt good. However, after a couple of years I realized if I was going to keep my marriage going, I needed to go back to Roswell. After I was hospitalized for kidney failure, we were forced to sell the Florida house.

In 1998 we had a home built in Florida as Hubby said he would retire after we sold our Roswell place. He lied, but *not* on purpose. He always *loved* working! He was very good at what he did, thank goodness. I didn't know *just how much he loved his job* until a few years ago. I thought he worked all those long hours because he *had* to. He loved inventing stuff the Ph.D.'s didn't seem able to do. He is not a golfer but enjoys hiking or reading. His retirement hobby is going out for breakfast and some small gardening.

About two months before closing on our Roswell place, Hubby announced that he wasn't ready to retire. We bought a townhouse near work in Norcross, Georgia. I told him the company should just give him a bed, microwave, refrigerator and bathroom with his office space. Ha, ha, ha. So, two moves at the same time, lots of drama with some big-time downsizing. It was fun shopping antique malls and good used furniture stores. It was time to change up.

In 1997 we purchased a lot near Jacksonville and had a

home built in a small subdivision. I was allowed to make changes. Unbelievable but true, I made 142 changes for which we paid extra. We closed in late 1998 before the sale of our Roswell property in 2000. I bought two new wicker and rattan sofas, some used white wicker dressers, a square table, and a couple of beds; plus I picked up three lamps at a local charity place. For a while I kept some of my clothes in our oven. Ha, ha, ha.

After selling the Roswell place and three years of my commuting (again), Hubby decided he wanted to cut back on work. About that time my good friend Faye loaned us her house in North Carolina. Soon we started looking for a mountain place. We chose a small, gray clapboard, minimal-upkeep place, about 2,500 feet up the side of a mountain, and three miles from downtown Franklin, North Carolina. We added a white picket fence (for our two Dals), wallpapered two bathrooms and our kitchen-dining area, and repainted everything. It was like a new house. After a couple of months, we sold our townhouse in a very competitive buyer's market. We lost several thousand but were grateful it wasn't more.

Now, thirteen years later, we are *thinking* of maybe selling our mountain home. We love North Carolina, but it is very hard on me to keep two places. Man, oh man, will that be difficult as I have furniture there that I still love. Unfortunately, both our boys are on furniture overload. For our new home in Florida, we bought new beds and camped out until we sold the Norcross place. We moved most of the Roswell furniture to the townhouse and then to North Carolina, selling only a few pieces.

Now you see, I have had lots of moving and practical decorating experience. I hope this advice will benefit you, darling. Sometime in 2022 you will be able to purchase my next book, *Decorating Isn't a Joke—Or Is It?* It will contain *lots* of helpful information and easy-to-use inexpensive ideas and some very expensive decorating suggestions for those that have more generous budgets. I really think you'll love it.

P.S. We decided to sell our North Carolina home and move to Florida full-time as it was getting to be too much work keeping up two homes. Now, we have to clean out the stuff we put in storage here. Ugh, I am reading AARP's book, *Downsizing the Family Home,* by Marie Jameson. She tells us what to save and what to let go. It was written about her personal experience of selling her parents' home. Another helpful book is *Clutter Free* by Kathi Lipp, which explains it is not what you are getting rid of but what you choose to keep. I am finding it very helpful as I am cleaning out my closets.

P.P.S. Sometimes getting rid of your stuff is painful. It is kind of like constipation, if you know what I mean.

Fun with Love, Passion and Sex

It is really lovely if you find someone who really loves you—the good—the bad and the ugly. I'm not talking about lust; I'm talking about love. There is a big difference. I feel a need to write this as I have young great-nieces going off to college. Since you have had very little dating experience, let me tell you about the birds and the bees.

I was a nerd in high school. I had to ask older guy friends to take me to my junior and senior proms. The one who had a crush on me gave me a hug and a kiss. A few months after graduation he took me out a few times. I guess he really liked me. He was from a good family and was honest, sweet, good-looking and hard-working. When he found out I was going to college, he said, "College will ruin you."

Yes, it did, but I feel in a good way. No one can have too much education. I'm not saying you can't be self-educated through deep reading and travel, but I am saying that college does change you; You learn about different cultures, and diverse ways of looking at life. You meet lots of interesting people who have various opinions on many subjects. Maybe your parents are Republican and your new friends are Democrats. You need to think for yourself. FYI, I have voted for some presidents in both parties and for an Independent. Voting is our right, a privilege and very important! There are a lot of people in our world that don't have the honor of voting.

What about religion? How do each of you feel about it? What are your beliefs? Are you of similar faiths?

One of my college boyfriends took up reading the Bible in order to understand it better, to aid him in his ongoing discussions with his buddies. I might have married this guy had the timing been different. He was very bright, attractive, a good friend, a wonderful companion, always interesting, humorous, and caring. We had similar backgrounds and we were both motivated to gain our degrees and do well in the future. He wanted to "do it" with me, but he was a true gentleman, as was my husband. There was no "pill" when I was in college. Although I was tempted, I resisted.

Today, I truly believe, passion gets in the way of getting to know the true person. If people are always having sex, they are only learning about each other sexually. Chances are they are not learning about the other person's thoughts and beliefs.

Back to love. As someone said, "What's love got to do with anything?" A lot! Love, according to Webster's Dictionary, is: 1: strong affection; 2: warm attachment; 3: beloved person. To me, love is always being there for each other. Watching what you say when he has made you very angry. To me, it is fixing dinner when it is the *last* thing you feel like doing.

How do you find "the one"? The answer is, very carefully.

If you have the opportunity try to hang out in a group of people, get to know a lot of gals and guys. Get to know what others feel about a lot of things. You can't very well do this if you are hopping on each other. Not easy these days. What Ye' Old Bitch (me) recommends is to go on casual daytime dates. Take it easy, really easy. Tell him or her that you want to learn all about him *before* any serious dating. You don't know him and, let's face it, he could be an overly possessive type—or worse, a potential Ted Bundy type. Think about that before getting frisky. Okay? *Always* let someone know where you are going and who you will be with. Please, please, please remember birth control beforehand.

You need to take a good look at yourself. Research has shown that if you don't love yourself, you can't really love someone else. What do you bring to a potential relationship? It is only my thoughts, but I feel each of you should know how to take care of yourself. This includes being financially responsible, no credit card debt, and able to balance your own checking account. I know several divorcees that broke up over money issues. Please be someone who values other things besides spending. Taking care of yourself also includes doing your own laundry, cooking and always cleaning up after yourself, as well as taking good care of yourself physically and emotionally.

Are you a half-empty or half-full type of person? How about your sweetie? Do you really like his relatives? Mama's boys can sometimes stay Mama's boys. Is his or her dad a hothead? How does he treat his mom?

Cleanliness, they say, is next to godliness. I am proud to say after sixty-plus years Hubby still takes a daily shower and always shaves. Ninety-nine percent of the time I put on makeup to look my best for myself and my sweetheart. At my age it would be a lot easier not to.

How does your honey treat kids? Is it possible he wants to make you his baby-making machine to trap you and keep you in a relationship? The husband of a friend of mine put a hole in his condoms so his wife would be forced to stay with him, and thus kept her from going to college. Surprise, surprise, she finally divorced him after years of public verbal abuse. Unfortunately, her children grew up to be verbally abusive to her, too. Now she sees neither. How very sad.

Is he or she supportive of the things *you* value in life? Is he or she trained to be a good income partner, or is he a guy who might end up with less education working for a big box store in a less than management position?

Do both of you know how—and are you willing—to clean up your space? I don't think I could stand being married to a slob, could you? And, cookie, get this loud and clear, you *cannot change anyone*! So, forget it!

Young lady, you also need to know that when a guy has sex, it is an event—*not* a commitment. Research shows most women bond to a man when climaxing.

Have questions about sex and passion? Go online to Roo Chat Bot where you can get honest, nonjudgmental answers to any of your questions.

THE single, most important decision that will affect your life, *ALL YOUR LIFE*, is who you marry or who you have children with.

I pray you might meet a good person who will always have your back, even though you won't agree on everything.

P.S. Save your real arguments for the big stuff, and don't go to bed mad. I pray that you will meet and marry someone who will be very supportive of your life's goals and will help you be all you can be. I hope you will be a loving and supportive cooperative partner. I pray that you will ask and thank God every day for guiding you towards a happy, healthy life.

Fun Saving Money

The American Association of Retired Persons (AARP) Magazine has some hints that can work for you at any age.

Replace land-line telephones with cell phone services that connect with your internet and television. You can trim over $500 per year.

Go for basic TV, giving up your cable. Difficult but *you will live*.

Cut your credit cards by using only one card for gas and groceries, hopefully a card that gives you back money. Missing a payment is horrible and can cost you big, big, bucks. If you find you are late, ask for a break, and you will probably get it but don't make this a habit. (To raise your credit score, pay early, and make an extra payment between bills.)

Make your meals at home and you will save a lot. You will be eating healthier and you could save as much as $600 in one year. To avoid waste, take your leftover produce, adding garlic, onions. Mrs. Dash and V8 juice, with one can of tomato (or other) soup and small cut-up potatoes. This will become what I call "yum-yum soup." To go with it, I serve cole slaw and make Jiffy cornbread, substituting orange juice for milk, which gives it a sweet taste.

Giving up costly name brand items such as full-priced cosmetics and toiletries could save you forty percent.

Clean out your closet, making a list of clothes you *need*. Check out charity shops for replacements. Most have clothes for kids too. If you and your kids are into brand names, you will have to look harder.

Avoid using banks that charge for your checking account; this could save you more than $144 a year. Avoid ATM withdrawal fees, which can be $4 or more, by buying items with a debit card. Track your balance to avoid having to pay as much as $30 in overdraft protection.

Gifts and gift cards can be purchased at a dollar store, bought in bulk. This may save you $100 or more a year. Be a bit creative by making up your own message. I often use, "Roses are red, violets are blue, I wish a special birthday just for YOU." For our fifth anniversary my hubby gave me an almost "too, too, too sweet" card (almost vomiting sweet). Bad bitch that I am, I wrote him the following message, "Roses are red, violets are blue, aren't you glad I married you?" I'm not a brain so if I can do it, so can you. Something I got away with, and still do, is to save cards I have given him and recycle. He doesn't remember getting them a few years before. Ha ha.

If you drop Amazon Prime, you may save up to $120 a year. You can still get free shipping when you spend $25 on most qualifying purchases. Check out walmart.com for their bargains on prices and shipping. If you feel you can't live without Amazon Prime, save by getting an Amazon Prime Rewards Visa Signature card. This would give you 5 percent back on anything from Amazon or Whole Foods.

If you have credit card debt, you need to *be responsible*! Get a small notebook and record every purchase made—even a package of gum. Record weekly in a larger notebook under titles like groceries, gas, car repairs, etc. You might want to color-code these. Make a game of it by challenging yourself, and/or your partner, to see if you can reduce your expenses. Remember, if you can't pay off your balance every month you should probably get one of Suze Orman's books on money management from the *library*. Make signs, listing your goals, and post them where you'll see them every day, like your mirror and refrigerator.

AARP has a free tool to show you how to pay bills and negotiate all your costs. Look up *aarp.org/moneymap*.

Fun Under the Big Top

Note: The following is from one of my son T.J.'s sermons.

In 1952, a twelve-year-old boy of color pondered at the rail cars that had stopped in the afternoon in his neighborhood of Baton Rouge, Louisiana. There were cars of animals, lions, elephants, tigers and beautiful show horses. The circus company had stopped in the railyard near the boy's town while waiting for the big tent to go up on the other side of the river.

The boy waited for his day-laborer dad to get home from helping put up the big top. He would be home soon as he wasn't allowed to be over there after dark; not that there were written laws but they knew their place. His dad, a WWII veteran, didn't want to be harassed or falsely accused; and besides, he was tired. The boy wondered what the circus would be like. It was traveling south to get away from the cold; unfortunately, it was as if the train brought the winter dreariness with it. The day was as gray as in London as his father had described from his old war stories. The grass of the Mississippi had seen frost and the leaves had fallen from the river birches, and the water reflected the greyness of the sky; the only color left was the dazzling hues from these exotic animals in their cages.

The boy peered around the train's caboose, watching the spectacle, peering into the eyes of several beasts. These beasts were trained but occasionally they would hiss, snarl or snort just to let their trainers know that they hadn't relinquished all of their instinctual power. The boy couldn't believe how many people it took to run a circus with all their stuff being off-loaded, trucked to the other side. To him the other side might as well be the other side of the world as he had never been there.

Even though he was already mature enough to know the real answer, he asked his dad if he could go to the circus. "I'm sorry, son, I really am. We can't get tickets. They sold out." His dad had stretched the truth so he wouldn't hurt his son.

Eighteen years later, the boy now a man, drove his very excited six-year-old son across the river. The man watched his son's wide eyes open when they entered the big top. It was then the man realized how much things had changed; through the diversity of the animals, the comic relief of the clowns, the joyous band music, the acrobats and even the circus hustlers; they had all come together to put on a show to put out their best to elicit smiles, amazement and laughter.

The audience too, now brothers and sisters from all backgrounds sat side by side to enjoy the show. People who wouldn't be worshipping in church together on Sunday were there together, on the same side of the Mississippi. The costume colors, the colors of the animals, their fur, the giraffe's long neck, the excitement, the music, the sounds of children laughing. The man realized this must be what heaven is like! And it is not monochrome. And he saw it through the reflection of the eyes of his child.

It was a journey, a national journey of conversation of what it means to be American with Christian ethics. It was a journey for this man's father, who served his country in Europe fighting despots and tyrants only to come home to inequality.

I first heard this story from my beloved former rector at All Saints. It was six years ago at a funeral for an elderly mother of a parishioner. I had served as the hospice chaplain for the deceased. I also knew her grandson Will. My son taught the thirteen-year-old Will in Sunday school. This past Sunday, a grown-up and very eloquent Will shared this story eulogizing his fifty-eight-year-old father Pat.

As much as my second love is marketing, I don't want families to participate in my "frequent *die*-er club"! I don't want repeat business! Will grew up in church and it showed as his eulogy was the best of the three as it placed the rightful spin of the resurrection of Christ during the celebration of life. The other two eulogies given by the yacht club and business partners shared things that I believe shouldn't be shared in church. It led me to an ethical dilemma; maybe they should be. Will's mother and Pat's widow is a friend of mine and I've known her for years, but this is where the ethics come to play. I had no idea that Pat was an alcoholic and that is what killed him.

It brought back memories of an on-call death visit I had made at eight o' clock in the morning to see a fifty-year-old mother dead, and she was as orange as a Florida orange. She also had the most serene smile on her face, as if ... she saw the face of God and she knew she was finally cured of her disease. I told her mother, a devout Baptist, that I believed that she was in heaven and she agreed, but the woman's husband and her teenagers grumbled in anger that it was all her fault.

That leads me back to Pat's eulogies this past Tuesday night. His movers-and-shakers friends, one of whom arrived by a Rolls, eulogized him by tales of womanizing, alcohol and worse, that his death was because of "personal choices." I've learned in the past that celebration-of-life services are not a place to air dirty laundry, and I would have never allowed this insensitivity to the family, inevitable shaming before a crowd of four hundred, but maybe I'm wrong. Perhaps we need to hear about the secrets that we all carry. Honesty seems to be in ever-short quantity in today's world.

As I said, Pat's widow is a friend of mine, and the All Saints rector and I locked hands with her and the three of us processed out so that she didn't have to leave alone. She had priests as human shields on both of her sides. I told her that she got to experience the trinity just then! She smiled and said yes. Before the service, I told her that we have something in common—that my ex-wife was named Pat and she died too, fifteen years ago. Her Pat died on July 13, and my Pat's birthday was July 12.

One of the things I've learned in life is to accept the messiness of humanity, the murkiness, as my Pat died from either an accidental drug overdose or suicide. I share all this as a public service announcement. That suicide and addiction deaths shouldn't be in the closet. That I would be glad to help anyone maybe in this situation, one without hope. I can attest there is hope. There are resources.

As I was driving home from one of my four visits to the thirty-four-year-old parishioner (who miraculously survived a suicide attempt), I was on the turnpike and had the top down on my convertible that I had then. I was enjoying the Florida clouds and feeling gratitude for being alive and for a purposeful life. It was my moment of peace like what the disciples were looking for in today's Gospel. Where else in crowded south Florida can we be deserted except in our cars? But usually it is not a Zen experience for me, but that day it was because the highway was serene. It was then that I felt my ex-wife's presence, and although not verbal, she was communicating to me that she was thankful for what I had done for our son; that she was behind my ministry somehow; and that she was okay or in an okay place. I wasn't used to God moments especially from a dead ex-wife, and it freaked me out so I put on the radio and the one song she hated came on; which was funny because I don't even know what her favorite song was. Out of billions of recordings, the one she didn't like came on and that was enough proof that she was talking and I was listening.

There is a key word in today's Gospel. If you had to pick out one theme, one word that best explains today's Gospel, it is compassion. "As he went ashore, he saw a great crowd; and he had compassion for them, because they were like sheep without a shepherd; and he began to teach them many things."

I have two questions for you. How does your God view the world? And how does your God ask you to view the world? Should our spiritual leader give compassion when our political leaders don't? It's a little ironic, but we can learn a little more about the word compassion from German. Their word for compassion is *Mitleid*; *mit* is with and *leid* is suffering, so "with suffering." The stories today are about real people who through their suffering were able to love and be with others, to suffer with, just like Jesus, the Sufferer-in-Chief! May God bless you and through his son, Jesus, help you through any of life's struggles.

Amen.

P.S. Fun Learning Patience from T.J.

Back in 2010, when I had a Buick Rendezvous, I was running late to church in Fort Lauderdale. Of course, I got all the red lights; then I was blocked by the Florida East Coast Railroad; then the draw bridge for the mega-yachts. Finally, I hit the accelerator on a downtown side street, normally empty on Sunday morning—only to see a girl basically taking her sweet time by doing figure eights with her bike in the middle of the street. After my ill thoughts (I probably vocalized them too) I looked down at XM radio and the name of the song was displayed: "Patience"! That's right, God was broadcasting me a message via satellite radio. I had a *rendezvous* with God. And incidentally, it wasn't the last time that I got a message through my car radio. Interesting?

Fun with Dalmatians and Disney

A day at Disney World was extra-special sharing it with 101 Dalmatians and one hundred other Dal owners. We were at Disney World to take part in a filmed parade. Disney was to use it in advertising the latest *101 Dalmatians* movie. We were dressed in nineteenth-century costumes. To the best of my memory the guys wore striped black pants, white period shirts with high collars and red bow ties and, I think, red suspenders. They wore black shoes with spats and straw hats. The gals were loaned white pantyhose and white lace-up shoes with two-inch heels. Our dresses were Victorian, made of a light cotton fabric in, I believe, a cream color. Rather a Gibson girl look with cute straw hats. The Dals were all on leads and behaved well. There were several Atlantis Dals besides my sweet champion, "Top Spot." We all had a ball.

Unfortunately, every time this movie comes out, people think they want one of those adorable little bundles of energy, not realizing that these active, darling, spotted puppies can become "big trouble" unless they are trained and get a lot of exercise *every day!!!* After all, they were bred to keep up with a coach for fifty miles. They are active, super-bright, "kinda like" a smart three-year-old child. They can be stubborn as well as destructive. My first one tore up a sofa when she was left alone. I quickly learned how valuable a crate can be when you are not home and as their bed (like a baby's crib) at night.

FYI: If you feed your dog in the crate or always give a treat when they go in, they soon are happy campers.

After the last movie, good breeders—including my vet friend and I—had real problems selling puppies. As a member of the Atlanta Kennel, I would receive calls from owners who didn't get their puppy from me and who clearly had regrets. If they wanted to "get rid of" the dog, I'd advise they take it back to the breeder who sold it to them. I told them that a good reliable breeder would always take them back. Of course, a lot of them came from pet stores and were unreturnable. The rest came from people who clearly just wanted "to make money."

Reliable breeders spend several hundred dollars having their puppies' hearing and health tested, plus shots. More experienced breeders can honestly tell you the health and personalities of the dogs for several generations. Our dogs come from generations of happy, healthy dogs. In most cases, you can see at least the mothers and some of the relatives.

We, meaning myself and others who have Atlantis dogs in their background, in several cases on both sides of the pedigrees, are blessed to have happy, healthy puppies, usually with good healthy coats and overall healthy stats. Some not-so-fortunate breeders deal with poor hearing stats, copper toxication, kidney problems, personality, coat, etc. Primarily, these problems have risen in the last fifteen years due to novices who breed for beautiful spotting. When these people line-bred, they got more of these problems, but they tend to win a lot as they are so pretty.

My friends and I have overall nice spotting in our dogs—sometimes a bit more spotting than I like. However, we have healthy, happy dogs; we don't breed to the big winners who have issues. Disney doesn't know everything, and that's why I am concerned about any Dalmatian movie that comes out. Not sure how I feel about the star Dal boy, "Captain," that carries my kennel name, being in the movie about Cruella de

Vil. His breeder and I went to a dog show together when he was about six months old. I saw him once since then, and yes, he did remember me.

I saw his litter at eight weeks. I had encouraged my friend to repeat a breeding. No patches, all dark eyes. All rims and noses were complete, nice open-to-moderate spotting, one with a bit more spotting, but no uglies. Beautiful possibilities, healthy and happy, no deafness or unis (meaning hearing only in one ear—not to be bred).

My friend had wanted me to take Captain, as he had so much fun playing with my Diva. But even though I am not super-smart, I knew it would be too much for me to handle as I saw them race around our back yard. If they were to run into me going as fast as they were, I would have been a pile of bones.

One should not keep a lot of males as sometimes they, like teenage boys, lose their cool, and things can get ugly. Captain seemed to be a mellow fellow but needed his own home. Although lovely show quality, my friend sold him to a California trainer who had trained the dog for the TV show *Frasier*. The new owner had flown across to Norfolk, spent time with Captain, purchased him, and soon he was sleeping on her bed. Less than a year later, he was in England making a Dal movie. I hear he is performing very well and that the trainer/owner adores him. Why wouldn't she? He is now three and has settled down. I just hope and pray Disney doesn't hurt our breed again!

Fun with Sex and Underwear

A friend of mine and I were in the Dollar Store, and while she finished up her shopping I decided to go ahead and check out. (Some would say my mind checked out long ago.) I had to wait as the checkout gal was helping someone find something. While I waited I looked around, and wonder of wonders, there were condoms near the chewing gum and candy bars.

I asked the checkout gal if they were a dollar. "Yes," she said. I said, "Wow, these would be fun to give to the right person." She laughed and said, "You would be surprised." (She was forty-plus.)

She went on to tell me about a relative who took her seventy-year-old mom to the Asheville airport for Mom's trip to Florida. Mom was going to see her boyfriend. Some family members came and gave Mom a farewell gift, a big bag with several condoms. Unfortunately, Mom didn't think it was funny. Her daughter—as well as my friend (who had joined me by this time) and I—thought it *great fun* and *very funny*.

A few weeks later I was telling my manicurist this story. She loved it. She then told me that her seventy-eight-year-old mother was dating and my friend found the "lovebirds" a bit much. She said that it really got her how much handholding, touching and kissing went on in the presence of family members. She said, "Young love is one thing, but older love can be disgusting." Maybe someone should tell them to get a room. I've heard some retirement homes have added "special" rooms for the old folks to hook up in. What do you think of this idea?

Okay, I'm asking, have you ever been kissing someone and been told, "Get a room." Really?

I've been told to go to my room by "Mama Dearest." Not the same, is it?

If you haven't read *Hold On To Your Panties And Have Fun,* you need to read how I have given girlfriends' husbands a rough time about "boxers or briefs." Those "brief" guys sometimes have "panty lines," as we gals call them. Actually, it depends upon how current the type of underwear is. The underwear people have gotten newer spandex/nylon combos that do wonders. They are so lightweight that lines don't appear and are great for travel as they dry quickly and take up hardly any space.

Guys' boxers were always made in cotton fabric but now are available in a cotton, nylon and spandex knit. The briefs, I understand, are even briefer.

Anyone want to do a research project and let me know the results?

When it comes to women's underwear, there are amazing possibilities. There are briefs, thongs, barely there, and some with holes where maybe there should be knit fabric. There still are the granny-type cotton knit which many gals still find comfortable. Then there are panties with super-support that suck in your stomach and kill you at the same time. I buy panties somewhat larger as I hate "tight underwear."

What I *really, really, really hate* are *tight bras*—or any bra after wearing it for hours. You gals understand this, don't you? Guess what? I found why old women don't like to go out at night—they have to wear a bra! When you get old, you can hardly wait to get home and get into leisure wear or PJs. This, Oprah, I know for sure!

Speaking of bras, did I tell you that I read where most bras used to have twenty-six different pieces of fabric? Now with spandex, the knit bras have fewer parts. But, damn it, after you wear any bra for a while, you are ready to go home. You're probably thinking "she hasn't tried the pull-over-the-head ones that look kind of like the top of a tee shirt." Yes, I did try one; it was hell for me to get on and off and I did *not* find it comfortable.

As most of you know, my first book has an attractive red cover with black panties with white polka dots. While I was doing an outside book signing, an attractive guy about fifty was looking at my book as his wife went into the bookstore. I told him he should buy the book for his wife. He looked at it, then said, "What kind of underwear do you wear?"

"I guess you would have to read the book," I said.

The jerk's very attractive wife came out as he hurried her away. She looked like she deserved better. She looked like her underwear was frilly … just saying.

P.S. There are underwear jerks I have dealt with at book signings. Among them, old guys with their wives, who have said, "Why would you want to hold onto your panties?" I answer, "I wrote the book for women, but I guess if you *need* to know that, then you need to read the book."

P.P.S. If guys had to wear super-supportive tight jock straps every day all day and work too, they *might* just begin to understand us. Oh, I think not, as most guys are totally clueless. Poor things.

But, hey, with the right underwear and the right guy you might have fun.

Fun with Cat Tails and Tales

A very good friend from North Carolina told me when she comes home from errands her cats always run to greet her. (I bet the husband doesn't come running.) I'm betting she feeds them. She is probably the person who cuddles them the most.

My friend Faye told me that her cat's favorite toy is one I made for him. I took a very small branch (about a half-inch in diameter), cut off the twigs and cut it so it was about eighteen inches long, making sure it was smooth. Then I took ribbons about eight to ten inches long and tied about five or six pieces on it in various places. She sits on the end of the sofa, resting her elbow on the arm turning the little branch back and forth. The cat has a good time bating those pretty ribbons and getting some exercise in the process. Since Faye is now ninety, she finds this "kitty toy" keeps her cat interested (actually longer than Faye) with a minimum of effort.

The following tale came from my friend and fellow author, Annie Keyes. It appears in her book, *Life Is Like Buffalo Breath*.

"My daughter's family has a pet kitty named Daisy. Daisy is an inside cat, a much-pampered feline. One afternoon, my daughter was outside; turning, she saw Daisy, sitting on the deck. Horrified that their inside kitty was outside in the cruel world, she softly called, 'Heeeere, Daisy.'

"To her amazement, Daisy jumped and ran off. After a few moments of unfruitful cat chasing, my daughter ran inside the house and panted, 'Help mama catch Daisy, she's outside!' The whole family ran out the door and started chasing the naughty cat. FINALLY, cat struggling in hand, they brought their pet inside and plopped the complaining kitty on the sofa.

"Yard weary and grubby, my daughter went to freshen up. As she walked into the bathroom, there lay Daisy, softly purring, stretched out on the rug. Needless to say, the unwilling imposter, still sitting on the couch, was unceremoniously plopped back outside."

Cat Jokes from the Internet (Hiss Hiss, Ho Ho)

Two female cats are sitting on the fence passing the time of day when a really handsome tomcat swaggers by and winks at them. "Oh my, did you get a look at that one?" one of the felines purrs. "I wouldn't mind sharing a dead mouse with him."

"Oh, forget about him," her friend tells her. "I went out

with him once, and all he did was talk about his operation."

A tomcat was heard yowling while running up and down the alley for hours. A neighbor called the owner and asked what was happening. The owner said, "I had him neutered today and he is going around cancelling all his engagements."

P.S. I understand males who have been neutered smell like female cats to other males.

P.P.S. According to my cat friend Cathy, "Cats sleep eighteen hours out of twenty-four. It takes effort to get eighteen hours of sleep per day."

P.P.P.S. To be owned by a cat is not only a joy, it is a gift—wish I weren't allergic.

Fun with House Plans

I have always loved house plans. I worked with builders in the sixties decorating model homes. Perhaps I should have studied architecture in college. Even knowing we aren't likely to build another home, I have occasionally checked out a book on house plans.

My readers and friends know I am addicted to Home and Garden television; however, I am sick, sick, sick of the Joanna and Chip *constant reruns*. Yes, they are cute and fun to watch the first time around, but it seems that Joanna tends to repeat her look over and over. But, hey, if it works—go for it. Joanna and Chip are working with people who have already bought their homes. Wondering if Joanna was forced to use the buyers' old furniture, how the rooms would look? Wondering after they move out the staged furniture and the new owners bring in their stuff, decorate it themselves just how wonderful it looks? Wondering how many people choose to buy the all-new furniture from Joanna? Wondering if this won't make an interesting series? I personally think Bristol and Audrey Marunde, who flip houses in Vegas, are more adventurous in their flips and do more overall interesting designs.

I love the "Property Brothers" and think "the brothers" do an excellent job. I love their decorating competition design show where they compete against one another.

I would like California's Christina and her ex, Tarek, Bristol and Aubrey, the Property Brothers, and Joanna and Chip to compete against one another in various categories like traditional, transitional, beach, New York glamour, Hollywood regency and art deco rooms. Wouldn't that be interesting? My guess would be the couple from Las Vegas would probably win the most rounds. Audrey seems to take the most color risks. From time to time, new faces and personalities do come on, which keeps me watching. The fixer-uppers all seem to open up their space to open up the house. It might be interesting if they weren't allowed to do that. Makes me wonder—how about you?

According to *Southern Living* magazine (March 2019) there appears to be a trend towards more separated spaces. One has to be super-neat and very organized to live in an open concept house; otherwise your home looks cluttered and messy. Surprise, surprise, surprise!!! Question, how many people keep a super-neat home?

It seems some people want spaces they can close off, while most people like a more open kitchen and family area. Sometimes there is a separate living room or study, providing for a last-minute guest or a quiet place to read or listen to music. Sometimes the study becomes a home office. This might work best if the room is close to an outside door should the owner have businesspeople who visit.

Our home was built in 1990, and we have an open window-like area over the sink that looks onto our leisure room where I do my writing and watch television. Our living room is to the right off the front door and can be closed off by the bifold doors for listening to music. I wish I had planned another door to close off the leisure/work room when Hubby is listening to loud music as I would like to hear my TV program without background music (especially loud violin music that drives me crazy). I remember hearing that a good man is hard to find, so I put up with it if it isn't too loud. Well, I don't call myself bitch for nothing, if you get my drift.

Our home is located in a community of homes built by the same builder. We were allowed changes, for which we paid dearly. I made one hundred forty-two changes. To accommodate my baby grand piano, I made our living room larger, taking space from a guest room. I also took nine inches from the guest room to make Hubby's office bigger. FYI, I sent the very helpful on-site guy steaks several times. I *try* to be nice and kiss up when necessary.

In order to have a coat closet, I took space from our kitchen. To make our dining room larger and more usable, I took about ten inches off the master. To make a walk-in closet I took space from the hall bath. In order to have an out-of-sight office, I took space from the master bath. This was a big mistake, which at some point needs to be fixed. I took out the tub, which I knew we wouldn't use. I had the bonus room expanded, which was smart. All in all, I love our home.

The change I really wanted was a front porch. A real architect could have figured out the changes necessary on the roof line. What we had was a sweet project manager. Ours were plan changes, not a true custom home. We would have had to go to a custom builder with a much, much bigger budget. Sometimes you have to be realistic about what you can afford. We feel blessed to be in a quiet neighborhood with nice, sweet people. While it is hard to think of everything, one floor plan change I made that I really appreciate is pocket doors, allowing me to keep dogs out of my kitchen / dining room. I planned for wider doorways to accommodate wheelchairs if needed someday, as well as higher toilets.

Later, after closing on our Roswell, Georgia, property, we were able to add a wall of bookshelves, crown molding, chair rails, a nice dining room chandelier and new tile floors. I took part of our laundry room and a tiny junk closet and designed a small bathroom. It has a shower, toilet and very small sink. This turned out to be a very handy guest bath with five sides, and mirror above the chair rail on three sides, which makes it look larger. Guests have told me that they really like it.

Twenty years later, our home is larger than we probably need, even though it works well with house guests. However, we now need to have household and yard help. Hubby thinks we should consider an assisted living place. Frankly, it scares the hell out of me as we have lots of furniture I love. Since we have been married over sixty-three years, we have accumulated way too much stuff. We still have a storage unit from our North Carolina home that we sold three years ago, that we are finally cleaning out.

Keep in mind, our garage is not wide enough for two cars, and Hubby thinks "his" car needs to be in the garage every night. It isn't easy downsizing. Hubby has agreed to allowing me three weeks to get stuff out of storage, clean out closets, and have a garage sale, with little or no help from him. Sweet dear man will be eighty-nine soon and never has liked helping me with projects. I keep telling myself "a good man is hard to find, so be grateful, old bitch." But I have to tell you that my good man could be more helpful.

Selfish me, I want to get some cash for a few of my decorating upgrades. He wants a charity to pick up everything and take it off our taxes. Will I ever see any refund if we get one? No, sir!

My other options: Find a flea market person who will buy most of the stuff or put an ad in the newspaper or on the internet. We'll see. I admit to liking lots of stuff so this won't be an easy time.

P.S. However, I am learning to let go of stuff. The book *Clutter Free* that Wendy gave me as a joke is actually helping me. It says to hold every item as you ask yourself: 1—Will I use this? 2—Do I really need it? 3—Do I really love it? As to clothes—I pass them on to two of my friends, and we sometimes exchange pieces.

Fun Being a Parent

Usually you don't realize just how difficult marriage and parenthood can be. Having children can be a joy, certainly, but, man, at times they can drive you crazy. Being a grandparent is most often easier unless you have a sorry-ass kid that didn't get their act together before becoming a parent themselves. If this is the case, you aren't done raising them either, are you?

The most important thing you can do to ensure you have happy, healthy kids is to avoid marriage until you are close to thirty. Know your future partner and his or her relatives before getting married. Then research your family genes. Have your or his parents or grandparents had any mental issues? Why are you asking that, Emily? By now you realize I am over eighty, which means, believe it or not, I have had lots of life experiences. I also have studied genetics and have seen how traits from ancestors are handed down through the generations in my dogs as well as our own grandson.

Grandson has not spent much time around his grandfather yet he is so much like him. I also see some of my less desirable traits. For instance, a lack of focus and difficulty handling more than one thing at a time. Face it, your kid will probably turn out to be a lot like his grandparents.

When becoming a parent, you have to give up, it seems, years of your life taking care of your children, while giving up your sleep. It is not easy; in fact, parenthood can be horribly stressing especially when you just get to sleep and receive a call from the police that your child has hit several mailboxes and the side of a house. And he has crashed the first new car you ever had. Oh, my—but we lived through that plus lots of motorcycle accidents. God certainly was watching over him and me. He was lucky I didn't kill him. Also, thank God he wasn't killed. No parent should lose a child, yet many do every year.

My advice is read books or watch videos on how to raise children. Do everything possible to love your child and let them know when they do anything that makes you proud—even making a peanut butter sandwich. Praise gets good results, while criticism causes resentments. I know, as I was never good enough for my mother.

According to Sarah Cain Spannagel, PhD, child psychologist at Case Western University, you need to follow the big three, "Touch, Talk and Look." Even older teenagers and adults still like to be hugged and have your undivided attention. They want you to be both emotionally and physically present in their lives by "being there" for them. It's very important to get to know their friends. "Like hang out with like." When I was teaching, I noticed that a new student soon was hanging out with someone like themselves. We know that kids need family time. If possible, ask them to bring one of their friends on your next outing.

Young people today like tech and probably spend too much time on the internet. Value their interests by asking them to show you their favorite sites or YouTube videos. Be present for your children.

You might want to check out a book written by family physician Deborah Gilboa, *Get the Behavior You Want ... Without Being the Parent You Hate*. Love the title, don't you? Maybe I would have been a better mother if I'd had a book like that one.

For your information, every mom who tries to be good at parenting has guilt—at least all the ones I have met. Just try really hard to listen to them, ask about things that interest them, hug them and praise the little beasts as often as you can.

Fun with Old Bags and Purses

If you are sixty or more, you might have fun calling yourself "the old bag"— or as I call myself, "the old bitch." This is good to remember when a much younger person who doesn't know you says, "How are you today?" I find it real annoying as they don't give a damn. They think they are being social when all it does is to make you think about all the crap your old body is dealing with.

In my case, it is a lot. There's forgetfulness, vertigo (once vomiting for five hours), arthritis of my hands, back, and feet, sciatica, glaucoma—no pain, just the irritation of putting drops in my eyes every night or go blind. Oh, yes, and neuropathy, which causes me to have burning, stabbing pain in my toes and feet in the middle of the night; now I keep this under control by rubbing Topricin cream before putting on my knee-high support copper-infused socks in the morning and a shorter version at night. I do twenty to thirty minutes on my stationary bike (a very sturdy one with back support I bought from HSN. for $200—very worth the money. I then do about ten minutes on a low push/pull machine, plus a ten-minute walk around my neighborhood, or the same time going up and down the stairs to our bonus room. It is a daily must do—unfortunately. I HATE, HATE, HATE any type of exercise, so why? I only do this to keep walking and hopefully to keep on having fun.

And speaking of fun, I have a friend who has lots of bags, some with their own bag. (These bags are out of my price range, okay?) I am really downsizing on bags, shoes, and clothes. I currently have only five purses, as I got rid of the rest.

I noticed I use the same one most of the time. More and more, I am trying to keep the numbers down. Recently I found an article that talked about purse-onality. According to this Woman's Day article, if you are a clutch carrier, you probably are a sophisticated, regal kind of gal. Maybe like Kate Middleton. You no doubt like delicate jewelry, and your style of clothes and interior design is subtle and simple as well as understated.

If your home decor and wardrobe are elegant and traditional, you are probably the center of your family and are known for being loyal, kind and trustworthy.

A gal who carries a tote is most often a charming, ambitious, and vibrant leader. Not only in her personal life but also professionally. Usually she has an energy that people are drawn to.

If you are an on-the-go busy person, an open-minded, curious, and adventurous gal who can manage a million things at once, you likely love crossover bags!

The hobo bag usually belongs to a free-spirited, creative type. It holds an abundance of all kinds of possibilities, from your lunch to a scarf, wallet, water bottle, your current reading material, and lots of stuff that you, your friends, or your kids might need.

Purses and handbags are always interesting and fun. But, hey, they aren't nearly as much fun as the gals who carry them, right? At least that is what this old bitch thinks.

Fun and Interesting Trip to Ohio 2019

In mid-May 2019, I once again boarded a plane to Atlanta on my way to Cleveland, Ohio, to go to the Dalmatian Club of America Dog Show. My trusty typist took me to the Jacksonville, Florida, airport. I went through security fine, but then I got into real trouble.

I had my large red handbag with the strap over my red Vera Bradley paisley carry-on (purchased on sale years ago), and I stopped to get water for my trip to Atlanta. When I left the restroom, I realized I didn't have my travel handbag. I went back in and tapped on the door of the stall and asked if my bag was there. "No," the woman inside said.

I was in *panic mode*! My allergy meds, a.m. and p.m. vitamins, my billfold with traveling money, charge cards and phone—all missing.

Someone, probably an attendant, said she had heard a TSA officer make an announcement about a red handbag. The agent looked everywhere and couldn't find it. He walked over to another agent and, like magic, it was found. Thank you, God!

I talked with these two TSA guys for a few minutes. One of them asked me where I was off to, and I said Cleveland but

I had to go through Atlanta. (If you hope to go to heaven, you have got to go through the Atlanta airport. Or is it the hell you have to go through to get to heaven?) I told the TSA officer I only had thirty minutes between flights and was very anxious about that. The TSA guy noticed my cane (I was getting over a recent vertigo attack) and suggested I ask my Delta flight attendant to get me a wheelchair in Atlanta.

This allowed me to meet a cool black guy who buzzed me from one part of the airport to a distant gate in time to make my flight. This young man told me he had recently graduated from college and wanted to go into broadcasting. He was currently doing podcasts. He was interested in doing one with me, after finding out I had written two fun books. What an interesting young man. He might be good in radio. I didn't tell him, but I know how limited the television openings tend to be.

On my way home, I flew from Cleveland to Detroit and again got a wheelchair as I knew how big that airport is, and frankly, I was exhausted from a long week of having too much fun and not enough sleep.

In Detroit I met a young girl whom I asked about her plans for her future work. She said she didn't know. I asked her what she was interested in. She didn't know. Her grandmother had tried to help her after she "messed up." (Whatever that means.) I went on to ask her what kind of grades she had in high school. "All A's." The special-interests testing had told her she was good at English. I asked her if she could see herself teaching. "Yes, maybe English."

"We always need good teachers and it is a chance to make a difference," I said.

Testing also told her she would be good at working with people. Then she said she hadn't thought about it before, but she might prefer nursing. I told her that good nurses are always in demand and she could make very good money while helping people.

With tears in her eyes, she thanked me for helping her to come to a life-changing moment. She told me she was glad to finally figure out what she should do with her life. I told her about New Hampshire University, a real college started in the 1800s that today is a not-for-profit internet college as well. Not sure if she can get a nursing degree or not. She said she wanted to be a psychiatric nurse. I am guessing she might have had experience being Baker-Acted.

I hugged her and gave her a tip and one of my books. I told her to listen to her grandmother, as I knew she must have loved her a lot.

Flying from Detroit to Jacksonville is a breeze as you don't have to go through Atlanta. (FYI—We lived in Atlanta for about forty years and remember how small and easy that airport used to be.)

P.S. Delta is really nice to old bitches.

Fun and Funny Memories of Our Sons

Our oldest son, S.C., who was due on our wedding anniversary, arrived a month early. The doctor said an enema I had taken brought him on. He was born breech, arriving feet first. Because of this, his head was round and beautiful; however, his nails and digestive system had not matured. But as I tease him now—it was the only time "he was beautiful." (He'll soon be sixty—OMG. How can that be?) S.C. was on a soy-based formula with bottles and nipples that had to be washed and sterilized daily. He vomited on me at least once a day for several weeks. In order to keep him clean I was using fifteen to seventeen diapers a day,

Hubby and I rented a tiny two-bedroom, one-bath house in St. Petersburg, Florida. It had a carport with a utility room and a wringer-washer. I hung my clothes on a clothesline. (I remember having twenty-five mosquito bites at one time.) S.C. had to be fed every two to three hours—day and night. Often, I would just get to sleep when he wanted to be fed. Actually, he was so hungry his doctor had me put rice cereal in his bottle. (Our second son's doctor put him on cereal at one week old, but I had to use a baby spoon.)

S.C. was a very alert, bright and happy baby. When he was about three months old, I started teaching adult classes a couple of evenings a week. (I developed an interior design class that proved to be very popular.) The day S.C. was eleven months old, he took his first steps with a great big grin. He had this "I've got the world in my hands" superior look on his face. (I was fortunate to get a photo.) When he was sixteen months old, I was teaching junior high home economics classes.

We were blessed to have a great babysitter/housekeeper. After I paid my sitter, I sent money to my parents to repay them for my college expenses. A year later, we bought a new home in Clearwater, Florida. I went back to teaching adults two nights a week. I was decorating model homes for two builders. I helped one of the builders by assisting his clients select finishes for their new homes.

Thanks to my mother-in-law talking with Hubby, I had a wonderful household helper a half-day a week. She kept the bathroom and floors clean and often got some of Hubby's white shirts ironed. This gave me more time to work part-time, be a mom and time to spend on my decorating projects. I made bedspreads, curtains, shorts and vests for our boys, as well as my clothes. I also refinished four or five pieces of furniture. I was active in the American Association of University Women, becoming program chairman when I was twenty-nine. Hubby and I belonged to a foreign film club and occasionally played bridge with other couples. We belonged to a swim club so that our boys could learn how to swim. We took the boys to church nearly every Sunday. Life was good!

At times the boys were challenges. When our oldest was about four and a half, a frightened neighbor called and told me our son had climbed up a tree in an empty lot. There were several families with playmates around his age. S.C. was going to nursery school two days a week. When T.J. was two. I took both of them one day a week. I would drop them off at about nine a.m. and pick them up about four p.m. It was "my day" to get things done at home and work my part-time jobs. It also kept me sane.

S.C. was a talker so when he got into something, he got quiet. He stopped taking a nap before he was two. T.J. was quieter; however, he was a climber. I had to put him in a twin bed at about eighteen months as he was climbing on top of his baby bed railing and jumping to the floor.

I remember when he was about twenty months, T.J. was jumping up and down about two inches from the edge of the dining room table, pushing on the chandelier. I got him down and put the boys and their toys on the screened porch while I was ironing nearby. Within five minutes, S.C yelled, "Mommy, T.J. is jumping on the porch table." I got him down and put them and their toys out in the fenced yard. Two minutes later S.C. yelled, "Mommy, come quickly, T.J. went over the fence." (The vertical fence was six feet tall.) He climbed up an orange tree next to the fence. No, he wasn't hurt, thank God. I brought the boys inside and had T.J. sit in a chair where I could see him as I finally finished Hubby's shirts. I think I aged about twenty years in those fifteen minutes. (Now he climbs on his roof to check it out.)

Soon afterwards we moved to California. S.C. was playing with another boy who had matches. They accidentally set a field on fire. The fire department was called, as I found out when the fire marshal came with S.C. to our front door. Needless to say, that was stressful!!!

When we lived in Los Altos, I was teaching high school full time plus going to graduate classes either at San Jose State or driving to San Francisco State. The first summer I taught half-day classes in Los Altos to help with expenses on our home projects. Fortunately, I had one of my students from San Jose High who took care of the boys during the week. Unfortunately, S.C. did not like her and was being very difficult, so I put him in a half-day private summer school program where he had math, reading and art. I was told he was the most outstanding art student of three hundred. (Later, in high school as a senior, S.C. scored, I believe, in the 99% range on the SAT test.) The next summer I drove to San Francisco for necessary graduate classes.

When S.C. was ten, he had to miss school because of a cold, and I got him a sitter. (His brother was in kindergarten.) After S.C. had this sitter for two days, he told his dad and me that the sitter was sleeping on the job and he didn't need her. He said all he needed was his dad's phone number so we thought, okay, we'll give it a try. (We lived in a very safe neighborhood.) We knew he was feeling better but not good enough to go to school. I fixed him a sandwich and there was fruit and milk so he wouldn't starve. In the middle of the afternoon Hubby got a call from our son and rushed home as S.C. heard voices outside and footsteps on our roof. His dad found him hiding under the long table skirt in our kitchen dining area. It turns out the power people were working on a loose wire on our roof. Thank God our boys were seldom ill.

When we moved to the Atlanta area in April of 1968, we found a newly built house. Coming from California, I expected the boys to be ahead of Georgia students; instead they were behind. I tutored them during the summer for about six weeks and got them up to grade level. Even though they didn't get straight A's I knew they were smart kids. Our youngest learned from his big brother's mistakes. I told S.C. that if he wanted to play down at the creek building his "dam" he had to learn multiplication. I had a record I would play about the multiplication tables. He hated hearing me sing along and still hates it today if I sing it. (Every few years I just have to have a little fun.) He learned his tables in quick order.

One Sunday, S.C. had trouble getting his shoes on for Sunday school. His feet were really swollen. When he took his socks off, I was *alarmed* at the cuts and sores, with pus. When I took him to the doctor, he was very surprised that S.C. had not complained of pain. He is like his dad as they both have a high tolerance. His brother, unfortunately, is like his mom.

Our Tucker home, northeast of Atlanta, was built on a hill. The kids had fun taking their sled or red wagon and rolling down the hill. T.J. and another kid went down together. Soon the wagon hit a rock or hole, tossing the kids. The older child fell on top of T.J., breaking his collarbone. Unfortunately, I thought T.J. was just being dramatic. Finally, the next day I took him to the doctor. Guilt, guilt, guilt! Life goes on ... *often* it isn't fun being a mom.

The boys loved our Dalmatian, Ladybug, that we purchased before leaving We soon added a half-sister, Love, who became Ch. Atlantis Love of Pacifica. A year later, we got Love's mom bred to Ladybug's and Love's sire, Best In Show, Am. and Can. Ch. Pacifica's Pride of Poseidon "Sy." We kept an adorable male who became Ch. Atlantis Bachaus of

Pacifica.

Dalmatians are an active breed and need an enclosed area to run. We had a fence and a couple of pens in our basement plus crates for them when we weren't home. Finally, having two litters and three adult Dals, we moved to Roswell about twenty miles away, where we had eight acres. It was surprising that our Tucker neighbors really did not want us to move. I never let my dogs bark unless the doorbell rang. I don't hate much but I do *hate to hear a dog's continuous barking*.

Once we moved to Roswell, the boys finally had more fun and more responsibility with the dogs. The youngest went to most of the shows with me. After giving up Boy Scouts, S.C. went to several Florida shows with me. Whoever stayed home took care of the other dogs.

The dogs were my outlet and distraction from work-related issues. I should have kept fewer dogs and spent more quality time with our sons. The older one, who I am very close to now, was a real pain during his teenage years. As Hubby was always working, I had a full load. The youngest was much easier to deal with and tried to help and please me, while the older one seemed to enjoy aggravating me. We all loved one another but the teenage years weren't easy. S.C. at seventeen or eighteen had two accidents in my small Honda (looked similar to a VW bug.) Finally, the second time it was totaled. He soon got his first motorcycle and since has had ten motorcycle or automobile accidents. If I look old, this is why. He was lucky he wasn't killed in one of these accidents, or by me.

S.C. started college at Georgia Tech but didn't last a year. He is very bright and has two U.S. patents and is now thinking of going back to college, at sixty no less. He will probably take online classes from New Hampshire

University, a not-for-profit school, which now offers in-school or online classes and degrees. (I have a very bright friend who teaches internet classes in law for this school. You might want to check this college out.)

    S.C. is a very talented artist but doesn't have much time to pursue it. He designed and built a bicycle. He and his adorable wife have a sailboat and have just bought a pine tree farm with a cabin on a gorgeous lake. Our son drives about eighty miles, round-trip, to work. (Until last fall, daughter-in-law had a large store where S.C. helped out during their busy times.) S.C. still has a number of motorcycles—I'm guessing five or six. Some he hopes to sell. I, the ugly mother, wish he would *sell them all*! At the present time they have a lovely three-bedroom house on a lake in Statesboro, Georgia. I'm lucky to ever get to see them. S.C. has worked very hard for his company since he was about twenty-five. He is very blessed to have gotten a great 401(k) policy with matching funds. He also gets, I believe, five weeks' vacation time a year. He is thinking of retiring, but needs to consider health benefits.

    At fifty-seven, T.J. is back in San Antonio, Texas. Even though he has three master's degrees, he is going back into real estate. He would have liked to be a minister; however, being older and gay, it didn't happen. (He has been with his partner thirty-plus years and is the father of our only grandson.) T.J. and I have always had a very close relationship. I am sorry to say I wasn't always aware of all the problems he had. He told me he was always the last kid to be chosen for kickball. How sad! He struggled with being gay, which I didn't figure out until he was twenty-something. Being gay is *not* something one would wish on anyone.

    Our grandson, J.D., left real estate to go to a graphic arts college, and is now working in south Florida. Grandson's very bright wife has an MBA and works in the advertising field analyzing data. I feel, as I helped raise him, J.D. is more of a son than a grandson. He is a very bright, handsome thirty-seven-year-old who his Gram adores. He told me recently that they are talking about having a baby. I don't ask or say much. I know J.D. would be a *great dad* as I have seen him with little ones. He didn't get that from me, but his dad was super with him. J.D. grew up with lots of problems that weren't of his doing. Life with his very sweet but needy troubled mom was difficult. She ended her life when she was forty-two. The Air Force and two caring dads, I believe, helped him become the wonderful caring sweet person he is today.

Thank you, God, for letting me see how good all my guys have turned out. I am very proud to know them, love them, and enjoy hanging out with all my family. Thank you, God, for helping me to encourage them, and thank you, God, that they have forgiven me when I screamed at them.

Fun with Old Dogs and Old Men

From personal experience I can tell you that old dogs are more fun than old men. Much, much, much more fun! Why? Old dogs actually listen to you—old men, not so much. Old dogs can still learn new tricks—old men, not so much. Old dogs still want to please you. Old men, seldom.

Okay, let's be honest, I have friends that are old men and am married to one. I've read that when a man gets to be sixty he just wants to do what he wants to do. That is, primarily—stay home and sit in front of the computer or television or read as he listens to "his" music.

I remember talking about this with an older female relative and her husband. I told them what I had read. She said she didn't think that was true. He grinned and said he would rather stay home. She looked shocked. (They had been married fifty years.) As I have gotten older, I have found that older guys don't mind going out during the daytime, but come evening they usually want to be at home. I've gotten a bit like that myself. Does that mean I am getting old?

Old dogs, as long as they get fed twice a day, are ready to go anywhere—anytime.

Speaking of eating, old dogs will eat anything—old guys are pickier. Old guys like real meat, preferably fresh, but not roadkill, please. Even though I give thanks for my old guy every day, I have never liked cooking. It is getting old, old, old!!! Thank God, today younger guys get in the kitchen and share the responsibilities. Old guys, only when they are in the mood or their wife is really, really, really sick.

When anyone gets older it is hard to learn new things. My old Hubby is not likely to jump through any hoops of any kind for me. He is not likely to hula-hoop either, while on the other hand, my old dog, who was eight at the time, had been taught a new trick. Our friend Buddy taught Diva the Dalmatian to jump up and into her crate in my van. I had tried and tried to get her to do it. Watching Buddy teach her was revealing. (It takes patience and really good treats and lots of praise.) Would Hubby jump that high for me? Forget it.

P.S. He doesn't wag his tail or rear end every time I come home, either ... Just saying.

P.P.S. But old men and old dogs share something in common—hair coming out of their ears and noses.

Fun with Underwear Again

Just when I thought I couldn't be surprised or shocked once again, I am. Why? On the front page of the Sunday

Jacksonville *Times-Union* is a photo of hundreds of people on a *cold* February day running down the street in their underwear. This was all for a good cause, "Cupid's Charity." This organization raised $18,900,00 for funding research for the Children's Tumor Foundation. All the donations went to this foundation. How about that? Very unusual—100%!!! A few of the gals wore leggings with bras. I wouldn't run down the street in my underwear if I could run. How about you? When you think about it, those gals may have had more coverage than those teeny-weeny yellow polka-dotted bikinis seen years ago.

Does anyone love support or sport bras? How about support or "suck your gut" girdles or shapewear? Not me! Sometimes for a special occasion I will wear a long-line bra with a very light panty girdle. Most of the time I wear black pants and tops that cover up the ugly lumps and bumps without heavy-duty support. Am I getting old? Yes—I've reached eighty-six so I am older, but I try to keep a "young at heart" attitude with gratitude for life and loved ones. Not always easy if I am having major back issues and using a walker or cane. Amazingly, I still get compliments on my attitude towards life, or my haircut, my big glasses or one of my striking jackets.

Did you know that in 1979 three women made the first sports bra from two jock straps?

When I was growing up, our choices in undergarments were very limited. We had a choice of white or black panties that were full coverage with elastic at the waist and leg openings. Keep in mind that I grew up in the country. We had JC Penney, Montgomery Ward's, and Sears catalogs, and fifteen miles away a general small department store. After college I lived in Dayton, Ohio, and after marriage, in Hartford, Connecticut, where there were large multilevel department stores.

It wasn't until the 1960s and the birth of "the pill" that fashionable underwear became available to the masses. I remember how excited my younger sister got over her days-of-the-week panties. I remember teasing her by asking if she did not know what day it was, unless she looked at her panties.

Now we have a huge assortment in panties. The "thong" with a low rise with minimum coverage, the "cheeky" with medium rise. The "bikini" with moderate coverage and a low rise. Then the moderate coverage, mid-rise "hipster." The high cut with mid- to high-rise is the "brief." The "boy short" has mid- to high-rise and full coverage. Plus, the seldom-talked-about panty that has an extra opening between the legs. Maybe for the too-anxious can't-wait types???

At holiday time, I received a catalog from the J. Peterman Company that had a drawing showing a guy lifting his leg up, showing guys how to put on boxers. It was a joke, people. To the right was a drawing of three pairs of boxers, plain blue, plaid, and striped, with the following: "British Boxers—The good news is, the Brits wear their boxers the same as the rest of us, so there is no learning curve. Boxers are easy, comfortable and less oppressive than some other tighties you might otherwise slip into. Some days you just feel like letting things breathe a bit. Made of pure cotton with real pearl buttons. Elastic waist and fly front with two-button functional closure. Made in England." Their phone number is (888) 647-2555 or you can reach them at jpeterman.com, should you want to pull up the drawings.

You can see by reading this ad, when I'm bored I'll read anything.

Some of you know how I like to tease men who I have known for a long time by asking them if they are boxer or brief guys. So far, these have been fellows I normally joke around with. Think I'll start asking the doctors I am seeing if they are boxer or brief guys. Hey, they ask me a lot of personal questions.

Wondering how they will react if they are going commando? Do you think they will tell me?

Have some fun and do the same.

I dare you! You could always tell them you are helping me do a survey.

Fun with Doctor Fill 'n' Drill

It is never fun to go to the dentist, but twice a year I get my teeth cleaned and a checkup. Dr. Fill 'n' Drill, a well-respected professional, can sometimes be a fun guy, especially if he is talking about his life.

He is very caring and gentle but has been the bearer of bad news two years in a row. You don't want to hear that you need a crown *re-done*. Last year it was two for me and I believe two for Hubby. Since these are $1,800 each, and we don't have dental insurance—we gave up all thoughts of any vacation. Thank you, God, for credit cards when you *need* them.

This year Dr. Fill 'n' Drill checked out my x-rays and told me I had to have another one redone, as tears ran down my face. When I was forty and had my first crown, a friend told me I would never have to have any more work done on that tooth. Wrong, wrong, wrong!

What Dr. Fill 'n' Drill told me this year was a real eye-opener. "The meds you take dry out your mouth, and in the aging process the gums pull away from the teeth, thus providing a perfect place for bacteria to grow decay under the crown." Finally, I'm told this, after brushing and flossing all my life and after spending $5,400 on my teeth in two years.

Now I am looking into dental insurance even though it takes a year for it to go into existence and is expensive. The shock of it all is just about more than I can handle.

After receiving the bad news, I had to pay my bill and was supposed to pick a date to get the old crown off. When the sweet receptionist asked me when I wanted to come in, I said, "I don't want to come in. I am going to weigh my options. Maybe I'll get lucky and die first." The poor gal was clearly stunned. In the background the office manager, who is used to my "naughty ways," just grinned.

I asked the dentist what would happen if I just had that tooth pulled. He said my other teeth would shift; therefore, if I wanted to continue eating steak, etc., it wasn't a good option. A week later, Hubby said I needed to get the crowns fixed. However, I really want to go up to North Carolina, as we were in Franklin for thirteen summers and I really miss my friends, the sunsets, and cooler evenings, and the "closer to God" feeling when I'm there.

Sometimes life is just difficult. I have a very small mouth and have had so much dental work through the years that I really have a *huge problem* making myself go. I know, I'm a dentist's worst nightmare. I am not patient; I require extra meds to get me numb. In short, I am a pain in the ass and, even *worse*, I *know* I'm a pain in the ass.

P.S. Please tell everyone you know to buy my books so I can pay off my big dental bills.

P.P.S. The only fun I have at the dentist office is seeing the young ones, who don't know me, left speechless.

Fun with Downsizing

If I get any more books on organizing and storage, some

of my bookshelves will break. Yes, I know how e-books work to save trees and put bookstores out of business. To me, there is nothing better than a small privately owned bookstore, preferably where everyone knows your name. As an author, these stores are the ones that are much nicer to us. They provide us a table and a chair so we can do our book signings. In exchange they get a percentage of the cost of a book, which is about what the author makes. They have rent and have overhead to pay. It is up to us to get as many books sold as possible if we want to be invited back.

Managing clutter is very hard for me. In fact, I feel it is my biggest difficulty in life as it involves lots of decisions. What do I really want to keep? Where do I put it? How important is this piece of paper, or book or piece of clothing, etc.?

Just a few minutes a day on downsizing, I hear, can bring us big results. Less stuff brings less stress. Maybe we need to remind ourselves of the difference between need and want. Maybe I need to figure out an appropriate reward for cleaning out. A party, perhaps—in my case, not food.

In 2019, we sold our summer home in Franklin, North Carolina. This was a very difficult decision but one that needed to be made. It was getting harder for me to manage keeping up two homes. Frankly, I was also beginning to be concerned about my husband driving on the curvy mountain roads. We both loved our twelve summers there with our glorious sunsets and mountain views. However, the thirteenth summer was a terrible summer for me. (Yes, I know it could have been worse!) My Hubby had gone to Franklin the first of June. I stayed in Florida to complete some home projects. I had fun refinishing several pieces of furniture and cleaning out the garage. I also got busy sewing new valances for our North Carolina kitchen and dining windows.

Day after day I had put in very long hours. I was acting like I was forty. This was NOT smart of me. I had a bone density test on May 5 and it was normal. However, on June 13, I bent over to scoop out a cup of dog food for Diva, and when I came back up I had a new pain in my back.

Long story short, I believe I cracked a vertebra that day and then, a few days later, broke it bending over to grab my heating pad cord to have it near my chair. Hubby came back and I began a summer of doctors' visits and surgery. He cooked, took care of Diva, grocery shopped, and was my nurse—he was wonderful! I was in such horrible pain—definitely not fun. Unfortunately, I was bitchy, bitchy, bitchy! Not in a good way. I really tried NOT to complain.

Finally, I went fifty miles to the emergency room, as pain got worse. I was hoping for surgery but was sent home with an appointment for ten days later with a surgeon. I had to come back in a week for a pre-op appointment. Then the surgery was a week later. Meantime, I was on pain medication that wasn't cutting it. The surgery was outpatient, and I should have been much better within a week or two. I was somewhat better, but my spine had never been good. I was born with scoliosis, then my upper back had broken bones from an auto accident. A normal, much younger person would have gotten over this in a couple of weeks. Finally I figured it out. I have a low threshold for pain so it takes me longer to get over surgery and pain.

Since our North Carolina house was going on the market, I had a friend finish the valances for the kitchen and dining area. We also arranged for a painter to come in and cover all the yellow paint with a pale grey.

Soon we got a good—not great—offer on our home. They wanted to close on August 15. We had to turn down their offer as I had an appointment with the surgeon the next day. The buyers came back a week later. We settled on a new closing date the end of October.

I was going to therapy before and after surgery and continued several more weeks. I had come off the cane but still took it with me as I felt uneasy on my feet. Hubby and I drove to North Carolina, leaving about 11:15 a.m. and arriving about 10:30 p.m. A very long, tiring 500-mile trip. I had wanted to stop and stay overnight, Hubby didn't. I spent a day and a half in bed. I was utterly exhausted.

Then came the sorting, getting rid of stuff, and the "Where are you going to put that?" "Do you really need more books?" and "Why are you really going to take that back to Florida?"—*every day*! Moving is a real test to any marriage, no matter how long you have been married.

This is what I found out, kids—creative types are a lot like me with our treasures. Clutter is there, be it books and papers, like me—plus art supplies, paints and paintings, plus fabric, dog pedigree papers, and photos. The organized accountant types will *never* understand the creative types.

Guess what? A former accountant type bought our place. They love our porch and mountain view. They have already planned some major improvements, new flooring and appliances. They plan to hold on to the wallpaper for a year to see how they like it. They already love our home and that's good enough for us. We like them, which helps us get on with our life.

Now we have clutter in the garage and storage area to try to organize. When I get this book and my next, *Decorating Isn't a Joke—Or Is It?,* done, I'll get rid of a lot of research papers and books.

Will I ever be clutter free? I keep trying—but seriously, I can keep a house clean, but not clutter free. Maybe when I get older.

P.S. A friend told me years ago that I was always in the process of getting organized; unfortunately this is still true. God help me, I don't want to be like the hoarders I see on television. No! No! No!!!

P.P.S. Update: Three years later and I have agreed to have the storage unit stuff brought to our garage. I have told Hubby I will need a month to get his garage back to normal. He complained, feeling I should do it sooner. I said, "It is better to under-promise and over-deliver." Can I do it on time??? Hope so. Sometimes life is a lot easier for my single girlfriends.

Fun with Animals

Sometimes—okay, often—I enjoy telling fun and funny life stories. Stories I witness or cause to happen or stories I hear about. A couple of years ago after an informal luncheon, I told one of my fun dog stories. When I finished, a luncheon guest told what I believe was a true story, but was *very shocking* to me.

The gal telling the story was a science teacher at a south Atlanta school. She decided to take a drive through some of the stately midtown posh Atlanta neighborhoods. When she saw a dead squirrel, she pulled over to the curb and took a hatchet out of her car trunk. She was walking back to the squirrel when all of a sudden, two armed policemen grabbed her and relieved her of her hatchet. They wanted to know what she was doing across the street from the Georgia governor's mansion with a hatchet. She told them her cat loved squirrel tails and pointed to the dead squirrel. Eventually they let her go, after telling her to leave the area. Since we lived in Atlanta for about forty years, I could picture the entire neighborhood. But, honestly, even though I have met lots and lots of people, I have never heard or met any woman—or man, for that matter—who carries a hatchet in their trunk. Have you?

Speaking of squirrels, have you heard the story of three very young and very small abandoned baby squirrels found in a nest in Maine? They were taken to Georgette Curran, who owned a local dog kennel. Since their eyes weren't open, they were probably under a week old. It turns out one of Georgette's dogs, a Chihuahua, had just given birth to two baby Chihuahuas. Norma, the Chihuahua, took the squirrels and raised them all together. They played together, nursed together and slept together. Homes were found for one of the Chihuahuas and two of the squirrels, while one puppy and one of the squirrels still live together and enjoy playing together at Georgette's kennel. How about that?

Another interesting dog story is about Isabella, a Golden Retriever, who nursed three white tigers that were abandoned by their mama at the Safari Zoological Park in Kansas. According to an article about zoo owners Allie Harvey and her husband, the golden nursed and cleaned up after the tiger cubs for several weeks until they were old enough to be fed. When one of the tigers would cry, Isabella would go to them to see what was wrong. Amazing, isn't it?

Cashew, an old dog, deaf and blind, was raised with two rescued kittens. She had a rope around her neck so her owners could easily lead her to her water and food bowls. Libby, one of the kittens, was soon pulling on the rope and taking Cashew to his doghouse as well as his food and water bowls. How sweet!

I also read about an abused Highland Terrier puppy, Milo. He was left with permanent damage to two of his four legs. Yet, get this, while at the beach with owner Lynda

Pomfrel, Milo jumped into the water and pulled to safety a much bigger spaniel dog. Way to go, Milo!

Tango, my son's Wheaten terrier, keeps the raccoon population down by watching out for them on their patio. If he sees any, he barks. When he is let out, he chases them. They usually escape, but not always. Sometimes Tango leaves a mess.

Years ago we had two Dals—Love, our first champion, and a male, Ch. Cloverhill's Comp-P-Tun Killa, (a cool name for a fun sweetie). While I walked from the dining room into the kitchen—maybe nine or ten feet—with dirty dishes, these two decided to quickly help themselves to a mouthful of Thanksgiving turkey. I yelled at them, grabbing the turkey, rinsing it off and putting it in the refrigerator to be recooked. All this happened in a very few minutes.

That year I had a Christmas tree with red and white balls, white angels and small white doves with white lights. It looked good until these two went bird hunting. They were obsessed. I had to remove all the birds. I have read where some Dals point. (I have seen many of mine do that.) Other Dals will hunt by flushing game. As I have said before, Dalmatians are fun, great dogs, but not for everyone. They need a take-charge owner who is smarter than they are. I'm not always, but I love them nevertheless.

My friend Wendy and I co-own a darling champion male, America Road Atlantis Harley Sportster, who we call "Harley." On a recent trip to see Wendy's son and his girlfriend, Harley decided to help her son to put his Christmas tree ornaments away by very carefully removing the ornaments one by one and giving them to him. All of a sudden, Harley lifted his front foot and started to stare at the side wall. It turns out the very old house they had just moved into had a mouse or two. Harley showed them where to put the trap.

P.S. My Dals have caught and killed rabbits and opossum, very quickly, when these creatures came into their country back yard. Not much fun to deal with.

Fun Life Lessons (How To Make Life Easier As You Age)

These are some of the things that have helped me and my older buddies:

- To prevent a fall at night, turn on a light or use a night light.
- Don't be too proud to use a walker or a cane when you need it. I keep a travel cane in my car so that if I get dizzy and need it, I could have someone get it for me.
- Take your underwear and pants to the bathroom and sit on the toilet to pull up your pants. (I keep a small dresser next to my toilet.)
- If you can possibly do so, get someone you can *trust* to come in and help with house cleaning.
- Take an AARP driving course to keep up to date. *AVOID* left turns unless done carefully at a light.
- Put front windows down to hear cars coming at blind intersections. Don' t drive after drinking. (As we age, we lose reaction times.)
- Be a smart driver. Don't drive on freeways if you have a problem merging or going the set speed.
- Give up driving if you don't feel secure. Consider the cost of your vehicle, gas and insurance. It is cheaper in the long run to take an Uber or cab. Many communities have senior transportation (free or low

in cost). Pretend you are a famous person with a driver. Take a book or magazine with you so you don't get bored—or your phone if you are a techie.
- You could lose all your assets if you cause a serious accident. (A former senior neighbor lost a lot of money after his car struck and killed a lady on a bike.)
- Make younger friends as you age. It will keep you young, and a younger friend might be willing to drive you *occasionally*. Don't take advantage of others. Remember, they have their own lives.
- Sometimes older people who may not be writing books, painting or working have too much time on their hands and tend to meddle in younger peoples' lives. Try very hard not to cause problems for others, or gossip—unless it is good news.

Hubby's hints for handling old age are the following:

— Try to eat healthy.

— Work as long as you can because you don't want to run out of money.

— Maintain your health by not smoking or over-drinking.

— Exercising (He rides a bike most days if not too hot or raining.) He also goes to men's newcomers' club meetings and programs given at the history museum.

Other friends have said how important social activities are—church, card groups, lunch with friends, hobby groups, etc.

Recently, I read where research has shown how important it is to keep pushing yourself to learn something new every year. Try to make a new friend, and take time to learn a new activity. Keep reading current books, or join a book group. Most important, try to have fun every day doing something or telling a friend a cute joke.

These are things I have learned from my own experience

and those of friends, including a few I have read about. FYI—pain is *not* fun, but I have found out a few things that help me deal with arthritis.

Acupuncture, I have found helpful. Recently I gave my trusty typist, Leslie, a session for her birthday. Leslie has arthritis and intense back and feet issues. She found it helped her and felt wonderful that evening after having the procedure. She is taking my advice and having at least two more sessions before deciding about continuing.

I have a couple of friends who continue to be in a lot of pain, but won't try it because they are afraid of needles. Girlfriend, these needles are the size of a human hair and rarely hurt. I have gone to probably eight to ten acupuncturists in moving around the country, traveling and on cruise ships. One gal from China told me that after treating a surgeon several times, he was sold. This doctor was building a new office and planned to have an acupuncturist on staff.

A Chinese acupuncturist I went to in Roswell, Georgia, told me that in China, before becoming a medical doctor a person is first trained in acupuncture. He also told me he has treated some of the big musicians who had come to Atlanta and needed treatment. I believe soon you will hear of more connections with Western medicine. (He called me "maxi-needles" as I believe he had inserted sixty at one session.)

Acupuncture, which is not always covered by most insurance, costs from $45 to $75 per treatment. It is not a cure, and neither are pills.

In talking with my local health food supplement store owner, I found "Cura Med," put out by Terry Naturally. It comes in 750 mg. On the jar it says "healthy inflammation response—superior absorption curcumin." It also says "up to 500 times stronger than turmeric." I do not take it daily; however, after a long, busy day I frequently have back pain (upper broken vertebrae from auto accident and lower back issues from birth) so I will take one if the pain is not too horrible, and two if worse. It dulls the pain, which allows me to make dinner. Walking doesn't seem to be as hard on me as standing and bending over.

I read a lot of health-related stuff and recently read about a practice called "earthing." According to Gaetan Chevalier, PhD, who is the Earthing Institute director, if you can sit, lie down, or stand barefoot on the grass or ground for fifteen minutes, it is like taking a vitamin. Chevalier believes you can absorb electrons from the earth, and this will then neutralize free radicals in your system to erase pain and boost energy. Not a bad idea to do in summer or in Florida, but what about when you have snow? Just asking.

I have found that chiropractic appointments help my back. However, I have to admit that when I do regular exercises, I don't feel the need to go there as often.

In dealing with doctor offices you need to make friends with people in the front office. (Try to remember people's names and faces.) You want to be in "the good graces" of the physician assistants. As you age, you may see them more than the doctors. The ones I have seen *seem* to know almost as much as the doctors. It doesn't hurt to give them a little gift once in a while. Flowers from your yard or a couple of cookies or a book you feel they might like should make you memorable. I try to be charming, if you can call it that, by asking about their children, grandchildren or their hobbies. Show interest in people, and they will remember and *maybe* like you.

When people ask me how I am, I usually say, "Fine for an old bitch," or "I am having fun walking around trying to avoid funeral expenses." Believe it or not, people grin, or laugh, and seem to remember me. Or it could be my big glasses.

My last hint is, try, try, try not to complain. Who wants to hear all of your troubles?

Fun with Hubby

Roses are red, violets are blue, let me tell you some of the things I adore about you!
- You are usually sweet and kind.
- You are still kind of cute.
- You are smart.
- You are fun most of the time.
- You are still capable of surprising me.
- You are still my rock.
- You are there or here when I need you.
- You can find stuff that I lose.
- You can fix stuff around the house.
- You help take care of me and for that I love you lots and lots and lots!
- You are my sunshine, my moon and my true love!
- You may be an old fart but you are my old fart and don't you forget it!

Fun on Mother's Day

Oldest son and daughter-in-love arrived from Georgia about 2:30 on Saturday afternoon. My typist friend, Leslie, and I had made all of us ham and Swiss cheese sandwiches. Soon, my beautiful daughter-in-love and I took off for our local upholstery shop while son visited with his dad.

Ms. B. and I went to look for fabric to reupholster the

sofa, chair and ottoman I had given S.C. before they were married ten years ago. When we had purchased this, we thought it was leather. It was—sorta. Turns out the Chinese, I believe, figured out a way to fuse leather scraps together so that it appears and *feels like soft leather*. Even though it was well taken care of, this leather fusion started peeling off its light fabric backing.

My friend's upholstery business closes at 3, so we didn't have much time. Ms. B. checked out a couple of samples. She will return the samples after they see how they look in their home. She will send the samples back and order the fabric. Ms. B. says they have a really good upholsterer in their area.

Soon Ms. B. and I were on our way to my favorite nail salon. This was a Mother's Day treat and a special bonding time as it doesn't happen often. After Ms. B. found a few cute tops at the shop next door, we did a quick trip to the grocery store. She and I like diet ginger ale to settle our stomachs, so I picked up a case. Ms. B. appreciates and is quite knowledgeable about wines and cheeses, so I told her we could get ten percent off if we bought six or more bottles of wine. She insisted on paying. She left four bottles at our house, which I appreciated and will save her favorite for their next visit.

We enjoyed the special cranberry nut cheese with a small glass of wine before driving to a riverfront restaurant where we enjoyed a tasty meal of beef and shrimp. None of us opted for dessert even though the choices sounded wonderful. I rarely eat all of my steak so I chose to take the rest home, along with the remainder of my large portion of steamed veggies, placing the container in my handbag.

Sunday morning, we went to a local resort for brunch overlooking the Atlantic Ocean, sitting in a shady area with a mild breeze. It was a delightful buffet with all kinds of breakfast items including bacon, best-ever fried potatoes, both link and patty sausages, waffles, pancakes, hot syrup, all kinds of fruit plus dinner items. Their roasted vegetables were really interesting. I had those and a piece of prime rib. My family had salmon and shrimp they raved about. There must have been five desserts. I had a small piece of dark chocolate cake with vanilla ice cream. I also had a bite of not-great cheesecake. Unfortunately, I feel they missed the boat with the desserts. Let me tell you, Ms. B.'s carrot cake or my milk chocolate cake or chocolate brownies are *much* better.

A surprising thing happened when I reached into my handbag for my glasses. I pulled out a piece of steamed carrot and some green beans that had fallen out of the container from Saturday evening. We all had a good laugh. All too often I just do dumb things.

While we were eating, I reminisced about past Mother's Days. Sometimes there were AKC dog shows in Athens, Georgia. Often, I would attend with a Dal houseguest and we would meet up with other Dal friends at the show. We would go to lunch, chat about our dogs, our competitions and our lives and just enjoy each other's funny stories. (You don't miss your kids as much if you are out having fun.)

When our boys were in their twenties, they would move out of the house and sometimes bounce back. Our oldest, S.C., and a friend were renting a two-bedroom two-bath home, when suddenly I got an urgent call. S.C. told me his housemate called him at work to say the house had burnt down—back he came. Another time I came home on Mother's Day to find him moving in again. Bad mother that I was/am, I said, "You've got to be kidding, you're moving back on 'my day'—Mother's Day?" At that time, he was easier to get along with when we weren't under the same roof. He didn't think he should pay rent—I did. Sometimes he was really good at avoiding me, coming and going when I was working or asleep.

I recently told his wife she had helped him to be a better son. Actually, I have always loved him, but now I *really* like and enjoy his company.

Thank you, God, our youngest went into the Air Force and has lived about six hours away except for a few years when they lived on the island. I remember him cooking for me Mother's Day or taking us out.

We are blessed to have good sons and a wonderful grandson. Thank you, God, for all of them and for my fun Mother's Day. In *Hold Onto Your Panties And Have Fun*, I wrote about T.J. and J.D. taking me to a Mother's Day drag queen luncheon and show—unforgettable. I would love to go back and sell those "girls" some of my books.

Aren't I blessed to have such a fun, interesting life?

Fun Being a Bad-Ass

Yes, I have fun being a "sometimes bad-ass." Today I connected with a grocery store manager. He appeared with a two-day beard. He said, "Hi, how are you doing?"

I answered, "Fine for an old bitch." (My standard answer.) Then I said, "They sell razors in your pharmacy section."

"Yes, I know but I also know I have one at home."

"Hope you use it soon," I said as he scurried away with a blush. Got you, buddy! I love blushes, don't you? (He has been clean-shaven since I gave him a rough time ... ha-ha.)

Have you read *You Are a Badass* by Jen Sincero? This book asks you to "stop doubting your greatness and start living an awesome life." This would be a really good book for anyone who wants to improve their life. Even though the book is an inspirational, God-based book, it does have an occasional "swear word."

P.S. I've read the Bible (maybe not as much as I should), but I have never seen where shit, damn or bitch are swear words and not to be used. But, kiddo, what do I know?

P.P.S. Whether you are you a bad-ass or a goodie-two-shoes, I love you regardless.

Fun with My Sister

On Labor Day evening, I got a call from our youngest son telling me my only sister, Gloria, had died. I had lost my only brother about three years before, our parents years ago. Now I am an orphan.

This brought back a flood of memories. From the time I was five, I was praying for a little sister even though I had a younger brother. Mother wasn't feeling well for most of her pregnancy. One day we had a babysitter taking care of us while Daddy took Mother to the hospital. Mother had a horrible cold with a really bad cough and was admitted to the hospital. Her doctor was hoping to avoid a miscarriage. I was in first grade and I knew our mother was in the hospital. I was really worried about her dying.

No one talked about pregnancy back then so I was clueless. Some relatives arrived to take my brother up to northern Ohio to stay with our Grammie and Grandpa and Mother's younger siblings. Daddy or a sitter would be at our house when I came home from school.

Gloria was a preemie weighing a little over four pounds. Fortunately the local hospital had just gotten their first incubator. After Gloria was born, a teenager from the children's home came to share my bedroom. She was there to help Mother with housework and the baby.

Gloria was my "living doll baby." When she was about nine months old, I was dressing her. I don't remember changing her diapers, but I was responsible for potty training. I was very protective of both my brother and sister.

I remember reading to her and playing school. I taught her how to sew when she was eight. Other memories include riding in the car together with my brother and sister on our family's Sunday afternoon drives after World War II. I remember playing cards, washing dishes while she dried, teaching her how to clean, make her bed and to say her prayers.

She and I went together to Sunday school and to 4-H meetings. I recall comforting her when she got upset. I remember our family watching television (NBC, CBS and ABC were our only choices) and our favorite show, "I Love Lucy." Our family got our first television, a black-and-white small screen, in 1952, when Gloria was eleven and I was seventeen.

After Gloria outgrew a crib, we shared a bedroom. This was a double bed for a couple of years. Her side of the bed was pushed next to the wall so she wouldn't fall out. Our parents bought us new maple bedroom furniture consisting of twin beds, a nightstand and dresser, and they painted our bedroom light blue. Our bedspreads were white chenille with white sheer curtains. The best part of the room was the ceiling. Mother had Daddy put star decals on the ceiling that glowed at night. It was fun for us to fall asleep looking at them.

Our family lived in my grandparents' home for several years, until my grandfather died. We kids went with our parents to look at farms, and they found one with sixty acres and a new Cape Cod white clapboard house, a garage and a concrete barn. Going from our grandparents' large five-bedroom home to a small three-bedroom, one-bath, was an adjustment. This house had a small living room with a kitchen and eating area. There were two small bedrooms with the tub bath separating them. (FYI—Yes, the five of us shared one bathroom.)

Our dormer room was cheerful with pink-and-white floral wallpaper. Mother added white sheers and curtains and the bedspreads from our former bedroom. Without air conditioning, it was very hot in summer and also very cold in winter.

I remember when I was a teenager and was overjoyed to receive a small radio for Christmas. This was a big deal back in 1952. I loved to listen to "Lux's Video Theater," which came on at nine o'clock on Sunday nights. Unfortunately our bedroom was over our parents' bedroom. I tried very hard to keep the volume down. Often Daddy would say, "Turn that radio off, now!" Of course I did. However, this taught my sister to sleep through anything.

When Gloria was eleven, I went off to Mary Washington College in Fredericksburg, Virginia. The next year I transferred to OSU in Columbus, Ohio. Like most college students, I was self-absorbed and very busy working one or two jobs and carrying a full load of classes, so seldom was able to go home. I would exchange letters with my sister, parents and grandmothers, bless their hearts. (Remember, I was the first grandchild on both sides of the family.) FYI—Long-distance calls cost about forty or fifty dollars for a five-minute call. We had a four-party telephone line—meaning four families shared one line. I got into trouble with Mother for listening in on our neighbor's interesting—to me—conversations.

Flashbacks of my sister include going to see our maternal grandparents at Christmas time when Gloria had a big bow on her almost bald head. She was born September 27, 1941, so she was three months old at the time. She was a charmer from the very beginning.

In elementary school, Gloria had anxiety over school. I thought maybe she wasn't quite as smart as Larry or me. She should not have gone to school at just six and especially without kindergarten. (In later years, Gloria kept her own sons out of first grade until they were seven. I believe all three of them were A students. I tried to keep mine in kindergarten but Hubby said no. Although our sons are intelligent, successful guys now, they were emotionally and socially slow in school as most boys tend to be.

I remember fixing my thirteen-year-old sister up for an OSU dance with a fifteen-year-old who worked at the movie theater with me. (We double-dated so she was safe, okay?) When Gloria died, I called my remaining college roommate who had been in our wedding with my then sixteen-year-old sister. She remembered her as being a bit shy, cute and very sweet.

My next flashback is of Gloria coming to see us while we were living in California when she had just graduated from Ohio State. I remember fixing her up with a guy I taught with at San Jose High School.

I remember going to her wedding when she was twenty-five. Gloria was a beautiful bride in a simple, long, elegant wedding dress and lovely bridal headpiece, which she designed and made. I thought her husband, Gene, was a "daddy substitute" as he was about ten years older. I based this on many summer visits of five to six days, and then a longer visit, at Mother's request, when Gloria had bladder surgery. (That was a very stressful visit for me as her husband complained if I didn't fix food the way "he" wanted.) I know Gloria and Gene loved one another, but I don't think he was an easy man to live with as he seemed to be always telling her what to do.

My sister, as a teenager, just wanted to be a secretary, get married, have a home and children. However, she decided to go to OSU and major in elementary education. She later changed to home economics, which she enjoyed. She got a scholarship for a year of graduate school at the University of Maryland.

After graduation she was offered a position teaching home economics near our family home and an offer to be an extension agent in Erie County in Sandusky, Ohio (200 miles away). Mother told me to encourage Gloria to go to Sandusky. Mother loved us but wanted us out of the house.

Gloria and Gene were fixed up by a co-worker (another OSU graduate). After a year or so they married. She worked a couple of years before they bought a farm and began redoing an old farmhouse. Soon she was stripping—not clothes—but lots of wallpaper. I remember her complaining because by this time she was pregnant and Gene wasn't helping her do this hard work.

Soon, it seemed, she and Gene had three sons, a newborn, a one-year-old and a two-year-old. (They were all born the same week, in different years.) Gloria was overstressed and overworked. She was *very happy* when all three were potty trained. She loved having them in her own home preschool.

In my opinion Gloria was a wonderful mom, perhaps overprotective. I remember when I was there and one of the boys didn't pass his drivers' road test. She was livid and felt the tester unfair. I said it might be the best for him, as it would make him try harder to be a good driver. Then she was mad at the tester and me. (Hey, I tell it like it is, like it or not.) She, I hear, called one of her son's professors about his schoolwork. (Who does that?) I believe she seemed anxious when her kids left home.

Fast forward—she was waiting and waiting for her oldest son and his wife to make her a grandmother. Finally, a darling little girl arrived near Gloria's birthday, followed by twins (a girl and a boy) about four years later. Even though they only lived an hour and a half away, she seldom saw them. She admitted to me that it was probably her fault. Soon her second son and his wife had a daughter. While this son was living in Cleveland, training to be a Mohs cancer surgeon, my sister was able to see her then seven-year-old granddaughter more often, before they moved to the Portland, Oregon, area. Later on she taught this granddaughter to knit.

Then at forty-five, her youngest, in Hong Kong, gave her a grandson. She became obsessed with her virtual "facetime" with this cutie. She got a visit from him when he was a year old and again at two years. With the twenty-plus-hour trip, wee one had trouble sleeping on a new schedule. I can only imagine the nightmare on the plane for the little one, his parents and all the travelers. I'm just glad I wasn't on that long trip.

Gloria was most always cheery when she answered her phone. While the boys were growing up, she managed their family strawberry business and taught the boys to weed and to pick strawberries while she dealt with the phone calls and people coming to the door. The boys learned good work ethics and this helped with their college expenses. When they got older, Gloria taught classes for young parents in a nearby high school.

Gloria made a big impact on many people. Her eldest told me she had recently put seventy-plus people on her phone's contact list. I remember her getting a special award for her extension work. Her students, friends and neighbors always spoke highly of her. Even though others thought well of her, she could be very caustic with family, more so with me. I loved her dearly even though I didn't always understand her.

Gene had Parkinson's for the last twelve years of his life. I know Gloria really wanted to come to our fiftieth anniversary party and he said, "No." This was several years before he died. Friends were willing to bring him food and check on him but he didn't want her to go for a two- or three-day important family event. Had it been me I would not have asked. I would have said I was going. She seemed to be very disappointed. I know I was.

Due to several moves, plus ovarian cancer, kidney failure, broken bones from an auto accident, and a busy life, I didn't see her for several years. When Gene died my eldest son, who lived near them for a few years, and I flew up to his funeral. My sister was in a wheelchair from a backward fall shortly before Gene's death. She was later diagnosed with *dysautonomia*, a nerve disease that continued to cause unexpected backward falls. From the time her husband died, she seemed to have more and more falls.

I went back to Ohio for the Dalmatian Club of America's Annual Show in Huron in 2015. This was held about seven miles from my sister. Frankly, I was stunned to see Gloria about a hundred pounds overweight. She was using a walker but had come to the door to let me and one of my girlfriends in. I was concerned she might fall. My friend, who had worked in nursing homes, told me that she felt Gloria was not doing all she could to take care of herself. I had to agree as she asked my friend or me to get her something when, had she reached over or stood up, she could have easily gotten it herself.

She was having someone with her most of the daytime. At night she had a phone with her and the couple who rented her attached house had a phone on their bedside table. Several early mornings they had to come pick her up after she fell in the bathroom. She broke several vertebrae in her back. I know from the auto accident how painful that can be. Gloria, like a lot of older people, didn't drink enough water, thus getting a number of bladder infections, as well as a number of other issues caused by lack of exercise and being overweight.

Somehow, she survived the turn-over and major drama with her caregivers. She had several hospital trips before she decided to give up her home and go to a senior care center. Gloria thought therapy there would help her. However, when there, her doctor son, who was checking on her, told me she wouldn't cooperate. She said she couldn't because it hurt. Yes, therapy usually hurts, but if you want to get better, that is the *only* way. After, I believe, another setback or fall she was a bed patient, no longer going to the dining room or anywhere. This was very sad for her and for me.

I tried to call her every five or six days, but it got harder and harder to talk to her. I would ask about the weather, her kids, and then tell her what was going on in my life. Not sure she wanted to hear how I was going out to Silver Sneakers, art and writers' meetings, meals out with my husband, etc. All the things she, seven years younger couldn't do, but I didn't know what else to say.

When she told me she was on her way out, I was shocked. A few weeks later I told her, "I know your life sucks but you have to do *the best you can every day*. I know it probably is very difficult. I, being older, should go before you."

In May when she answered the phone, she said, "The funeral is going to be June 14th." I said, "Whose funeral?" Gloria replied, "Mine."

I said, "You don't get to plan your funeral, God plans that." In July and August, she set dates, but finally she gave up and I guess put it in God's hands.

Her death, although expected, was still shocking to me. When I last talked to her, she sounded so normal, her voice was strong and for the first time she asked me about my life and what I was going to do about the two teeth the dentist wanted to crown. I even got a laugh out of her when I told her that his receptionist asked when I wanted to come back in for the crowns. I told her, "I don't want to. I need to figure out my options and maybe I'll get lucky and die first."

Even though I had spoken to her three days before she passed, I had been thinking of her all day. I was just about to call her when I got "the call" that she was gone. But I still think about sitting in church with her when we were both young, singing the song they played at her funeral. I remember the fun playing house with our dolls. I remember playing card and board games, which she adored. In later years I recall long phone calls when we would catch up on our busy family times.

The sad, sad end of a special life and the end of an era. I have no one to call me "Sissy" anymore. I often think of things I want to ask or tell her.

Fun Favorite Bible Verses and Quotes

- How good and pleasant it is when God's people live together in unity. (Psalm 133, NIV)
- This is the day which the Lord has made. Let us rejoice and be glad in it. (Psalm 118:24, NASB)
- This is my commandment, that you love one another as I have loved you. (John 15:12, NKJV)
- A joyful heart makes a cheerful face. (Proverbs 15:13,

NASB)
- The Lord is near to all who call on him. (Psalm 145:18, NIV)
- Keep me safe, my God, for in you I take refuge. (Psalm 16:1, NIV)
- Rejoice in all the good things the Lord your God has given to you. (Deuteronomy 26:11, NIV)
- All things are possible to him who believes. (Mark 9:23, NKJV)
- And, lo, I am with you always, even unto the end of the world. (Matthew 28:20, KJV)
- Whatever is true, whatever is honorable, whatever is right, whatever is pure, whatever is lovely, whatever is of good repute, if there is any excellence and if they are worthy of praise, dwell on these things. (Philippians 4:8, NASB)
- God didn't promise days without pain, laughter without sorrow or sun without rain. But he did promise strength for the day, comfort for the tears, and light for the way. If God brings you to it, He will bring you through it. (Unknown)

More Fun with Dr. Good As It Gets

Unfortunately, I have had lots of contact with doctors lately. Today I had an EKG and a report from my internist. He said I looked terrific and looked much younger than I am. I said, "Well, Sonny, your eyesight is really going."

He laughed and seemed to be in a really good mood so I asked him what was going on with his hair. He asked me why I asked. I said there were curls in the back and he needed a haircut. He said his wife was in charge of his hair (whatever that means). I told him I feel sorry for her having to put up with him. Turns out she is out of town taking care of grandchildren in Hawaii. He said he didn't feel sorry for her; in fact, he said he was jealous. I told him I am glad my only grandchild is thirty-three.

I asked him if he had time for a "Dr. Up Yours" story. He said, "Tell me." Dr. Up Yours is a patient and friend of his and now a retired colon specialist.

I told Dr. Good As It Gets that I had run into our doctor friend at the grocery store while the manager, Gary, who is like a nephew to me, was lifting some dog food. I said, "Gary, this is a guy who has seen more of my body than anyone."

Dr. Up Yours, with twinkly blue eyes, said loudly, "Yes, I did her last colonoscopy and I remember it well!"

I replied, "You are a real bad-ass, aren't you?" Both men joined me in laughter as I hugged Dr. Up Yours. As my friend Gary and I moved on, I said, "Maybe I should have had my bottom bleached!"

Gary asked me if people really bleach their buttholes. I told him that I have heard that some people do. He grinned and blushed. Gary and I have been buddies for several years, after I found out he lived near us north of Atlanta, Georgia. He gives me a hug every time I see him. Gary had bought a copy of my book, *Hold On To Your Panties and Have Fun* for his ninety-something aunt, who I hear loved it.

I love small towns where a lot of people know each other! Even better, they love having fun together.

Fun in the Kitchen

After several months of Hubby's cooking, I decided it was

time to get back in the kitchen. I told Hubby I would make a casserole (the base would be a mix). Hubby was pleased. I was surprised, however, when he said, "You are not going to bake it over 300 degrees, are you?"

I replied, "I'm going to follow the instructions on the box."

Then he went on to say, "Don't put the temperature over 300, as when you do, it gets crusty around the top, and I don't want the pan soaking overnight in MY sink."

Of course, what did I do? I put the oven at 400, like the box said, then lowered it to 350 when I put the casserole in.

To make my casserole I start with a scalloped potato mix with cheese. I only use one and a half cups of boiling water, about one-third of the cheese mix, as I am allergic to cheese, and one-half of a small can of canned milk. I then add chopped ham, pork, or hot dogs, and about one-half of a chopped green, red and yellow pepper. To that I add one-third cup of chopped onion and half a can of petite tomatoes. I might add about one-third cup of frozen peas or mixed veggies. (When I reheat this dish, that has four servings, I add the rest of the milk and tomatoes.) On top I will sprinkle pepper and a light sprinkling of Mrs. Dash seasoning.

I don't want the casserole to be dry or have too much liquid. I start the oven at 400 degrees; then when I put the casserole in, I drop it down to 350 until bubbling with a bit of crust.

Hubby had been wonderful, fixing all our meals for about four months. Due to my back issues it had been difficult to stand and, due to the coronavirus in 2020, we'd been eating at home all the time.

I went back to my comfy chair and watching television. After about fifteen minutes I checked my casserole. I noticed the oven was now set on 300. I turned it to 350 again. I sat down to watch HGTV again. Ten minutes later the oven was once again at 300. I turned it to 350 and set the table, giving each of us a side dish of cold whole cranberries from a can that had cooled in the refrigerator.

I finally turned the oven off, noting that again it had been set at 300 degrees.

What my friends find amusing is that neither of us mentioned changing the oven temperature then or since. That is how you avoid arguments when you have been married over sixty years.

Fun with Vertigo

Darn it anyway, the older you get the more you need to exercise, eat healthy, and see your internist.

Thank God for Medicare and good supplemental insurance. (We use AARP.) However, it often costs more out of pocket than expected. As you know I like to joke around with doctors. I also let them know that I have a Bachelor of Science degree and placed, I believe, thirteenth in the state of Ohio in biology. I let them know, in a roundabout way, that I think their job of helping their patients is not easy, as every case is different. Sometimes I throw in that I know that it is called_medical *practice* for a reason. Clearly, I am not a darling cooperative client. But guess what? Even though I am less than charming I usually get a grin or laugh. All the doctors seem to remember me and greet me with a smile—maybe because I'm not boring.

The summer of 2017, I had taken a really wonderful hot shower. I put my underwear on in the bathroom and grabbed a top and pants from the closet. When I went to bend over to pull my pants up, I suddenly found the room was spinning

400 or 500 miles per hour. I screamed for Hubby as Diva, my Dal, sat very anxiously at my door. I grabbed my wastebasket and started vomiting.

I told Hubby to call 911 and to get me a basin. Soon two very cute EMTs arrived and put me in a kitchen chair and carried Ye Ol' Bitch out to the ambulance, and off to the hospital we went. While one guy drove, the other was hooking me up to fluids, checking my heart rate etc. I asked him what he thought the problem was. He replied—vertigo or a stroke.

At the hospital if they think you have a *heart-related problem, they get to you really fast.* A lovely doctor, a natural blonde, forty-something, came into my room. I knew her but wasn't sure from where. We finally figured we had met at physical therapy. She had been there for her knee, I for my back. After a CAT scan, MRI and blood tests, she told me it was vertigo. Five or six hours later, after receiving anti-nausea meds, I was feeling better and could go home.

I used a walker and was told not to drive for a few days. I was referred to therapy. I tried to get an appointment at a clinic about one mile from home. They didn't have an opening. I was able to get in a few miles away and was amazed, when I got there, to know my therapist. He had come to our house after my knee replacement. Surprise, surprise, surprise! He remembered me, even though it had been five or six years since I had seen him.

I later gave him my first book and told him I had written about him in my upcoming decorating book, *Decorating Isn't a Joke—Or Is It?* My therapist grinned and said, "Really?"

"Yes," I said, "however, in my pain-medicated drug state, I had remembered you being cuter and taller." He laughed as he blushed. "Yes, and I thought you had blue eyes, not brown."

He had me lie on a table, putting my shoulders on the

edge. Then he raised my body up and had me turn to the left. After holding my head lower than my shoulders for a few minutes, he carefully raised me up, then did my right side. This is called the Epley maneuver and seemed to help *some*.

Fast forward to the fall of 1918 and again I was feeling dizzy. Again, I was sent to therapy. In addition to the Epley maneuver, I had an exercise where I wore a wide safety belt while my therapist held on to me as I walked with my eyes closed. I went to therapy several times and thought I was better.

Vertigo is weird in that, apparently, if you have a crystal problem in your ear, the Epley maneuver usually solves the problem, or at least for moment. In late February I was having problems with my balance again. By mid-March I had two vomiting attacks within two weeks. With the first, Hubby took me to the hospital—same-old, same-old meds and fluids and six hours later I could go home. The last attack came on so fast I ended up staying home, vomiting eight times in five hours. I really thought I was dying.

My internist sent me back to therapy, as well as to an ear, nose, and throat doctor, and on to a balance center where I had my hearing checked. I found out that my right ear has perfect hearing while my left had lost a lot of function. That could have been caused by an ear infection after a bad cold/sinus infection in 2016. This they felt was the cause of my hearing loss.

A three-and-a-half-hour balance test was planned six weeks later to get to the root of my balance problem. I found out that the clinic near me had a vestibular therapist and so I began going to see her. My old therapist and the new one both felt it wasn't the usual crystal problem.

The testing was done fifty miles away. I had my friend and typist take me as I had to have someone drive me home. I love Hubby but his driving would have made me more anxious than I already was—if you get my drift.

The hearing doctor told me she would have a really cute guy run my tests. I was told to not wear makeup, eat very little and to bring a change of clothing. The testing was scheduled.

When my name was called by a cute thirty-plus-year-old guy, my friend and I went in together. As I passed the hearing doctor, I said, "I thought you were going to get a cute tester." She laughed, and bless his heart, he laughed too. While my friend watched TV and read, I had a really miserable time. The first series of tests involved standing on boards that moved up and down while the walls of the room as well as the ceiling moved. I almost vomited as I began to lose my balance. Fortunately, the tester kept me from falling.

All of the testing required my wearing a big helmet. Not sure if it measured eye or brain movement. Then the next tests were done while sitting as I watched videos to make me feel off balance. The last tests were done lying down while watching colored circles fly by. I thought for sure I was going to vomit. (Someone later told me she passed out at therapy.) The testing was *really* irritating; then I was told I would have to come back for the results.

I had some fun teasing the cute tester, so when I came back, I brought him one of my books. He grinned and thanked me as he gave me a big hug.

I continued to go to local therapy and chair yoga and Silver Sneakers when I wasn't too dizzy to stand. Unfortunately, none of the doctors seem to know what causes vertigo.

Selfish me—I had planned a trip to Ohio for the DCA dog show and a couple of days to spend in Medina with my nephew's adorable family. What do I do? I had been prescribed a med by the local ear, nose and throat doctor. One doctor at the balance center told me she never seen it prescribed before. Get this, one of the side effects is dizziness!

I asked my pharmacist to check my meds and tell me If I could take 25 mg. meclizine more than just before bed. (A good pharmacist knows all about meds.) So, on the Saturday before I was to leave, my pharmacist told me I could take it up to four times daily.

With determination, a cane and meds, I was able to make my trip. I had to change planes in Atlanta and experienced dizziness when the plane was taking off. Had I not been on meds, I probably would have vomited. The balance center person told me it was to be taken as an emergency med only and to lie down after I took it. I was told the meds could make me dizzy and make most people sleepy. It seems to slow me down, but I was walking and talking and leading a sort of normal life. I am just glad I was smart enough to question my pharmacist. I have found you have to be alert and ask lots of questions. Doctors want to do the right thing. Clearly stated on my medication guide, that this medicine can be used as a *preventative*. Why didn't any of the four doctors I saw tell me?

The doctor at the balance center said, "We knew something was wrong with you but we didn't know what." I said, "My friends have been saying that for a long time." My internist told me, "Eighty percent of people who get vertigo get it again, and you have proven that you are in the eighty percent."

I can sometimes go without meds all day long; however, if I feel a bit off, I take the medicine. Wouldn't you if you were afraid of falling? I was advised to continue with therapy, which I did, feeling better but not normal.

Hubby agreed to go on vacation to North Carolina where we had a summer home for many years. I was thrilled. While I was there, I visited a therapist. Then a miracle of sorts happened when I went to see Dr. Tracy, my natural physician and acupuncturist. She placed two small black seed tapes on each ear, so they were back to back. She told me to pinch on them every time I was feeling dizzy. Thank you, God, for leading me back to Tracy. Every time her name comes up, I hear more wonderful ways in which she has helped people.

If you have a similar problem, I would suggest going to a very experienced acupuncturist. You can find one by calling around for one that has been doing acupuncture for at least fifteen years. I have gone to at least five in moving, etc. I have found a couple of younger but good ones on cruise ships. I find that they can't cure everything but they have helped my back issues as well as other aches and pains. You have to go at least three times to find out if it will work for you. Since most insurance doesn't cover this, you will usually have to pay $65 to $100 a visit. Consider that this works for a lot of people; otherwise, they would not remain in business, right?

I know vertigo is a frequent problem for the elderly. I do not wear seed tapes daily; however, I used them for about six weeks as I continued with meds at night and my vertigo exercises when I remember. I consider myself fortunate and blessed that I have had no vomiting vertigo in over a year.

I include this information as I went to six or seven professionals *before* I got help that made me feel like a real person again.

Take care of yourself, I need my readers.

Fun in the Mountains — Vacation 2019

Dorian forced us off our lovely island. A three-week trip to North Carolina was planned to begin mid-September; however, due to Hurricane Dorian we moved it up a week. (Hopefully, you're *not* like I am and try to get your home all neat and tidy before you leave town.) To clean and pack at the same time, I was pushing myself and was very stressed. Knowing we could possibly lose everything, I took more things. I just had to take my new top, jacket and pair of Isaacs's blue flowered sneakers.

We stayed one night at our son and daughter-in-love's home in Statesboro, Georgia, after stopping to see their new farm. Their new property consists of lots of pine trees, a beautiful lake, and hunting cabin. S.C. gave me a tour of his acreage on his BOSS (a four-wheeled enlarged golf-cart type of thing). How cool was that? Then he showed me his electric bike he designed and built. At six-foot-six, he looked like he was on a kid's bike. He plans to use it as an art object and probably will hang it on one of the cabin walls.

Bad girl that I am, I told him the rustic cabin looked like a "before" on a home and garden television show. I suggested they add a deer head and maybe a rattlesnake skin. *I was kidding* but I got the idea that he thought that would be a cool look. He usually shoots one deer a year and has it processed for their freezer. Hubby never hunted nor did my dad, even though my brother did.

The next day we left for Franklin and the beautiful mountains we love so much, knowing at our ages it might be our last trip. We arrived there about four p.m. on a warm Sunday afternoon. The temperature was still in the nineties but dropped down to mid-sixties that night. I was expecting it to be up a ways, but was surprised and not thrilled at the one-lane, very curvy mountain road. It was paved but had several blind curves. Driving up the mountain reminded me of years ago, when I had driven almost to the top of Pike's Peak before my daughter-in-law begged me to turn around.

We had not been to Franklin since we sold our small mountain home in October of 2016. Franklin looked much like it did when we left. While we were there for three weeks, I went to my old weight group, WOW (Watching Our Weight) twice. It was really fun seeing old friends and meeting new members.

Suzanne, who owns Books Unlimited, allowed me to do three Saturday book signings. Writing books is not easy and not fun, but book signings to me are *joyful*! I love meeting new people and telling them about my books. I always ask if they are local or visiting. Most of the buyers were from the Carolinas or Georgia, a couple from Franklin. After seeing the book title, *I Hate Porta-Potties, Sprinkles and Tight Underwear*, some of the buyers wanted to know why I didn't like "sprinkles." I said, "They are a waste of sugar that could have gone into chocolate!" They laughed.

The first day we were in Franklin, we went to our old grocery store, where I ran into our former neighbor. We were both surprised as hugs were exchanged. A few days later we met for lunch with our hubbies. It was fun catching up on all the neighborhood news. Wherever we went, it seemed I ran into people I knew. When I went to the art gallery where I was a former member, I was asked to join other painters to paint and later for a meeting.

I had hoped to get a painting done while I was there; however, I was not able to complete it. Painting is *not* like riding a bike. If you haven't painted for a couple of years, it takes a while to get your mojo back. I wanted to paint a flamingo on a black background. My, oh my. (I was able to purchase a 24-by-24 wrapped canvas for $25 from an artist I met. Unfortunately, I didn't plan well and had to buy more paint and new brushes for $30). I spent two days working on "the flamingo" before giving up and repainting the background black with colorful tulips. In the past I have done several tulip paintings which came out very well. The third day I went to the gallery, I worked and worked on tulips.

Another artist loved it and said I should give it to her. No, sorry, it was not good enough to hang anywhere. I was going for a field of tulips; however, it turned out to look sort of like wallpaper. Now my plans are to start all over—ugh. See how much fun painting can be?

Now that I am home, I am back to trying to finish up this book and trying to do fall house cleaning – not easy. The painting will have to wait. Sometimes life can be fun and sometimes not so much. However, I had a great time seeing old friends and acquaintances. Just experiencing the clean mountain air, eating fresh foods, and visiting the quaint mountain shops was fun and unforgettable. Loved, loved, loved it!

Fun Helping You Get A Job

You need a "stand-out resume." Since many employers read resumes on smartphones, you need simple, sharp bullet points. Be specific about your track record and achievements. Avoid cliché comments like "proven track record" or "successfully" or "results oriented."

You need to take stock of all your talents, not just those you used in your last position. What do your family and friends say your talents are? You may benefit from making a list of things you liked about your last job. Make another list of favorite classes or activities you have enjoyed. Look within yourself to find abilities that you have that you may have not used in past jobs. Make a list of what you have found out and what you might want in a dream job position.

Time to update your photo and get connected on LinkedIn and other employment sites. Reach out to classmates who know your true worth. Go to all the network and community employment opportunities available. Give your card and keep others. Give out help to others, and help will come back to you.

In the meantime, keep up a normal routine, keep up your appearance through eating healthy food and exercising. Every day, study the businesses in your area to find a company where you would like to work. Research these companies, inquiring about job openings.

There are lots of good books. I saw one at the airport that I thought might be interesting, and it is *Lose The Resume, Get The Job* by Gary Burnison. I would also check out Louise Kursmark's book, *Career Changes*, and *Finding A Job Fast By Using A 30/60/90 Day Plan* by Peggy McKee. In addition, look into *What's Next? Finding Your Passion and Your Dream Job in Your Forties, Fifties and Beyond* by Kerry Hannon. (FYI: She writes for *Forbes* magazine and is AARP's jobs expert.)

P.S. I love the affirmation and the inspiration offered by Florence Scovel Shinn in her book *The Game Of Life*. Pray for the right job as you give thanks—it is on the way.

Fun with My Paternal Grandparents

My dad's parents were very frugal and rarely spent any money. They were born in the 1800s. My grandfather's relatives had come from Scotland and originally were called McClellands. At some point the Mc was dropped. Then, according to Dad, one of the L's was later dropped, as a relative didn't want to have thirteen letters in his name.

I met a couple about twenty years ago here in Florida that

had the same last name. I do believe we were related but they pronounced their name Cleland, like Leland, while my family pronounced it like McClelland without the Mc.

My grandmother's maiden name was Moon. I met several ladies in Georgia married to Moons and all told me the same story I had been told. That was that the Moons came over from England (mine in 1682) and settled in the Carolinas, some moving to Virginia and on to Ohio, others to Georgia. A friend of mine and I were talking about our family trees. Later he dropped off a copy of his background, and it is probably part of mine. While in Virginia, two or three Moon girls married McClellan or Cleland guys. I have been told that the Scottish relatives go back to Viking times in the 1400s. Maybe that is why I am sometimes a bad-ass?

After talking to my cousin, I found out Cholie, my grandma, was born in 1883 and died at seventy-seven. Grandpa Armasa L. was born in 1874 and died in 1947. They were married in 1907. My dad was born in 1910 and died in 1991. His brother was about two years younger. My mother was born in 1911 and died in 1998.

My parents truly loved one another and for the most part were loving parents. I believe our Cleland grandparents loved us, but they were not huggers like my mother's relatives. This was probably in part due to their being of the Quaker religion.

They were farmers, and Grandpa would often, after working, come in to get a glass of water and go out on the porch and sit in the rocking chair. He could be really grumpy. My sister was terrified of him but I wasn't. One time he fell asleep, woke up and said, "Who's snoring?" I remember laughing and saying, "You, Grandpa!"

I don't ever remember him hugging me as my grandma did. My cousin doesn't remember him much but does remember talking to him and sitting on his lap. I told her it was because she was younger and cuter. I thought about it and realized she didn't spend time with him at the end of his life like I did.

After Grandpa Cleland died and my parents bought a farm fifty-five miles away, we seldom saw our grandmother, cousins, or friends in Martinsville. My mother had a problem with having to move away from friends, as did I. Soon Daddy went back to work for the U.S. Conservation Service. He would meet with farmers and would teach them how to make their land more productive, as well as helping them with engineering draining issues. He loved his work and it was less hard on his body than farming. My dad was born club-footed and at his mother's insistence had surgery at three months, wearing a brace on one foot and leg until he was five. He always had a special lift on special shoes. I know he seldom complained but we knew he had leg, foot and hip pain all his life.

When Grandpa died, I had to go stay with my grandmother for a while. She taught me how to use her treadle sewing machine. I was afraid every night that she might die and I would find her dead body the next morning. Without television, we would play board games and go to bed early. She was always very sweet to me. I remember her driving down the lane every morning and evening to milk the cows. I frequently hung out with her. She also checked on her chickens. One of my jobs was to gather the eggs. Often the hens wouldn't want to leave their nests and would peck at my hands. I truly hated them. However, I loved the cows.

Both of my parents' families were hard workers and well thought of by neighbors in their communities.

Fun with My Maternal Grandparents

My mother's mother we called Grammie. She was born in the 1800s. She worked as a seamstress, making dresses for wealthy people before and after marriage to Grandpa Frank. They had six children—my mother the first daughter, and I, the first grandchild. Soon others would arrive so then I wasn't "that" special.

My memories of Grammie are all positive; however, my mother and two aunts felt Grammie had an acid tongue and wasn't always fair to them. I just remember her wonderful food. She would make strawberry shortcake with two or three layers, squashing berries and placing them between the layers. This was served warm with fresh homemade whipped cream. Yum, yum, yum!

Grammie and Grandpa always had to struggle. They purchased a farm with an older house that unfortunately burned down when my mother was four. They had to start over. They would have had more family support if Grandpa hadn't had a falling-out with their Catholic priest. This priest had told him he needed to give more money to the church, and I guess his siblings agreed with the church. My mother had been brought up Methodist. I'm not sure if Grammie and Grandpa went to church. I certainly don't remember going to church when I visited them. However, I believe my aunts and uncles as adults took their families to church.

My grandparents were both very hard workers and, with their children's help, built up their strawberry and vegetable "farmer's stand" business. They had a dairy cow and probably a beef calf raised for food as well as a good flock of chickens for eggs and food. Grammie canned vegetables for the winter.

My Aunt Helen, who was about eleven years older than I, wrote a book about her life and said how cold their house was in the winter. Snow, she said, came through leaks around the windows. They had to go to the outhouse or use a "pee pot" (chamber pot) at night, which was emptied and cleaned every morning. All the girls were taught to sew and made their clothes, including underwear for the entire family. I believe the men were able to purchase overalls, but Grammie and the girls made them shirts.

This meant, until after World War II. all the girls had was two or three dresses each. I remember visiting at Christmas time and taking a bath in a big horse trough filled with water heated from the fireplace. When I was about ten, my grandparents enclosed a side porch and installed hot water, a bathtub and a real toilet.

One of my favorite memories of Grammie was the time when Grandpa drove us to Wadsworth, Ohio, where Grammie took some of her egg money, I'm guessing, to buy me a pair of Shirley Temple black patent Mary Jane shoes. I wanted Shirley Temple shoes forever, but my Quaker-born conservative Daddy had said no. This was the best gift ever when I was nine or ten years old.

Another memory of Grammie is her painting the living room a rich kelly green—WOW. Maybe she is the one who got me interested in decorating and color. I know she had white lace curtains and, I believe, new beige furniture with green throw pillows. The floors were wood with some kind of large "want-to-be" or real oriental rug. I remember how proud she was of this room.

Years later when attending her funeral, I remember telling my Aunt Emily that I bet Grammie would have loved the funeral home's kelly green walls. Aunt Emily said that

Grammie had picked out "that" funeral home because of the "pretty green walls."

Maybe you will remember my writing about my Grammie coming to me years after her death—her face surrounded by clouds—after my cousin Ada Marie, her namesake, died. Grammie said, "Ada is all right. She is with me."

Years later, my Dal Atlantis "My My" came to me too. I heard her bark. (FYI—Every dog has a slightly different bark.) I was putting Tex outside when I heard My My's bark. I looked out to see a small cloud floating across the backyard the size she had been. Both times it shook me up. Regardless of what you believe, I believe in life after death.

I wasn't around my Grandpa Frank much as he was always out working in the barn or in the field or going to Akron with a load of fruits and vegetables for farmers' market. My cousin Lowell, who grew up nearby, told me that Grandpa would give him and his younger brother homemade wine or sherry when they were eight or ten—shocking. I'm sure Grammie would not have approved of that.

My memory of him was a time when he ate poison ivy, telling us some people got sick from this. I don't think he did and, as I remember, I told Grammie. He loved his kids and grandkids. According to Aunt Emily, my mother was his favorite and if someone gave Aunt Emily a gift or she got a new dress, and Rose, my mom, wanted it, Grandpa made Aunt Emily give it to her.

I do know my mother was a jealous person, from overhearing her conversations with Daddy and what I personally witnessed, so I believe what Aunt Emily said to be the truth.

It was wonderful to be loved by my grandparents and my aunts and uncles.

Fun in Cleveland

Hubby and I left home at 7:15 a.m. on Sept. 27, 2018 (my sister's seventy-seventh birthday). Unfortunately we were on our way to her funeral. We flew out of Jacksonville, meeting up in Atlanta with our oldest son and his adorable wife. Lordy, lordy, lordy, can that airport get any worse? I had forgotten how long it is from one end to the other. Yes, they do have trains and, yes, at my age I could have asked for a wheelchair. But, hey, I'm not a wimp, so Hubby and I walked and walked and then walked some more. Finally, we all boarded a plane for Cleveland, Ohio.

We arrived in Cleveland about 3 p.m., where our son picked up our rental vehicle. Son is six-foot-six and, believe me, the Infiniti was taller. I understand it weighed over seven thousand pounds. Lots of leg room, which is always good! We drove to the hotel in Medina, located near my sister's oldest son. I keep asking if he is fifty—yes, I know my M.B.A. nephew is just forty-eight, but I also love teasing him. He has such a cute smile. My nephew and his sweetheart of a wife have three teenagers—all are great kids!

On Friday, we went with the Medina nephew to visit the Rock & Roll Hall of Fame in Cleveland, where we met up with our youngest son and his spouse. The exhibits are all very well done. Interesting to me was the fact that *almost all* of the rock stars were or are very short, some not much over five-foot-four. I'm not a huge rock-and-roll fan but I thoroughly enjoyed seeing all their outfits. You could easily spend several days in this place, it is that interesting.

After several hours we left to go to lunch. Our tour guide nephew suggested a German restaurant. It had a lovely brick exterior, and along the street it had about ten tables with potted plants. I told nephew I had been coming to Cleveland since 1954 and this was the first "awesome day" I had ever seen. It was balmy and a delightful seventy-degree day with a light breeze. The sun was out, a rare occurrence in my experience. We all loved the wonderful German food, which is often hard to find in the South.

Next we headed to the Cleveland Museum of Art. This museum is very large, wonderful and free. Not sure where the money came from to build the art collection and the continuing expenses of utilities and the many employees. All my family seemed to really enjoy this experience, except getting separated when it was time to leave, with no cell service. I spent my time revisiting the large Monet and other Impressionist paintings. I felt sorry for our son having to drive back to Medina in the "going home" traffic. No one complained about anything, thank you, God! It was a wonderful shared time.

That evening we went to nephew's home for a fun takeout meal. I got to hang out with my sister's twin grandchildren, age fourteen (boy and girl). The older sister, eighteen, was off to an "all-important" football game with her "besties." Their mom told me she was going to feed the kids and then the adults could go out on their deck to eat. I told her, "No, no, I'm eating in here with the kids." They were really adorable. They seemed happy to have spent time with their "bad-ass" great-auntie. I love bright, sweet teens. They were so polite with me, but, *more importantly,* with each other (almost so sweet you might want to puke). How refreshing. I loved my two when they were teens but I don't remember them as sweet. (They are now—thank you, God!)

My sister, in healthier times, would have had a fun day with all of us. I *know* she would have wanted us to spend quality time together. Hubby and our sons had not seen the relatives in probably twenty years.

Niece-in-law offered me a house tour, but frankly I was plain worn out so didn't get to see everything. I told nephew that my youngest and I thought their home looked like a "Leave It to Beaver" house and neighborhood. Nephew thought it a real compliment, as it was meant to be. What a sweet, cute, loving, all-American family.

After a very long fun day we headed back to the hotel. The morning came too soon. We brought our luggage down before breakfast and were soon on the road.

I came from a loving family, consisting of my parents, my younger brother, sister and me. My parents lived until they were in their eighties. My brother died about four years ago. Now I am the oldest living relative on both sides of my family. Maybe I've lived longer because Hubby got me out of Ohio. I love Ohio in the summer, *I really do*, but I am happy I don't have to face snow.

We arrived at the funeral home about 10 a.m. As I came in the door, a younger fifty-something gal said, "Emily." I had not seen this gal since she was about fourteen. I had called her about five or six times when I couldn't reach my sister, who had told me this gal was like a daughter to her. I do know she visited Gloria at the nursing home two or three times a week. I remember her living across the road from my sister. (She and her husband bought my sister's house.) A real sweetheart!

As per normal, I couldn't help but cry as I sat on the front row with my sister's grandchildren. They took it all better than I. The casket was open, and we were about ten feet away. Our youngest, an Episcopal priest, did a great job. One minute, people wiped the tears away; the next minute he had us laughing. As I was coming out of the room, I saw Gloria's younger friend again. She gave me a big hug, then really broke down. I just hugged her for several minutes while we both cried. After the graveside service, all were invited to a nearby restaurant for a lovely cold buffet lunch. I had brought some of my jewelry that I passed on to family members.

Soon, our son said we needed to leave to get to the Cleveland airport for our flight back home. We all went back to his room to quickly change clothes. This was a riot as four males, daughter-in-law and I all changed in a hurry. None of us wanted to travel in our funeral clothes. As I, "The Old Bitch," changed in their bathroom, they changed in the bedroom. You don't want to see the sights I saw. We were all laughing.

Two hours later we arrived at the airport and took off for Jacksonville, arriving home about midnight. After a very long day that started at 6 a.m., it was *so good* to be home again.

I look forward to returning to that area for the annual Dalmatian show at the Saw Mill Resort in May. I hope to hang out with the teens and their parents. Northern Ohio is so beautiful in May with tulips, daffodils, cherry and dogwood trees in bloom and the beautiful fresh green grass.

I was sorry Gloria's other sons didn't get into town until late the evening before the funeral. One is a Mohs cancer surgeon, married to a Ph.D. who teaches at the college level. I was disappointed to only have a short chat with their fourteen-year-old daughter. The other son just received his Ph.D. in psychology. He and his wife, who does marketing/advertising, have a two-year-old who had visited Gloria in June. They live in Hong Kong, and after twenty-two hours one way on a plane a few months before, this son came alone for the funeral. I got a chance to visit with him a few minutes at lunch. I probably won't see him again, as I would have loved to go to Hong Kong when I was twenty, but now it is too crowded and China is changing things. Sorry that they don't live closer.

We hope both families will come to visits. However, now that my sister is gone, my life is not the same. I try to focus on the fun times I had with her but it isn't easy. I feel so sorry Gloria isn't here to enjoy her nearby Medina grandchildren and their parents, whom I love dearly. I often think of things I want to tell her.

Fun with No Pity Parties

In a moment, events can drastically change your life, and mine has changed several times. No one is expecting a doctor to tell you that you need surgery to remove a five- to eight-pound ovarian tumor. (I believe it was the talcum powder.) I had lost a cousin to cancer only a few years before; thus this was very stressful. I decided I wasn't going to put my body through treatment. Fortunately, I didn't have to.

Years after my cancer scare, we sold our small farm near Atlanta. On July 3, after having my van checked out (I always have it completely checked out before any long trip), I was on my way to our new Florida home with a van full of furniture. It was a very hot day on the three-lane south Georgia highway. Many vehicles were cruising along at high speeds in all three lanes. I slowed to seventy. I was in the left fast lane. I wanted to move over to get off at the next exit for lunch. However, all of a sudden, I heard a loud noise. I was having difficulty holding onto my steering wheel as my van shook. I wanted to avoid hurting anyone or getting hit. I put on my brakes to slow my van and move off the highway.

Suddenly my van went down fifteen feet into a ditch, and I quickly found myself heading up towards oncoming traffic. I was frantic!!! To avoid a head-on collision, I turned the steering wheel too quickly to the left. A moment later my van flipped over, crushing in the driver's side and my body. Needless to say, I was in trouble. Even though I had on my seatbelt, my head cracked the windshield. At the time I didn't seem to notice much pain or blood.

The paramedics arrived quickly, breaking the windshield. One of them asked me if I could move my legs, feet, arms, and hands—I could. They tried to pull me out and could not. They pushed a small guy through the right window. He pushed on my butt as others pulled me out. I was worried about my older Dal, "My My." The door on her plastic crate had come off. Her crate was sideways and she was standing up looking around. Someone took her to the vet while I was taken by ambulance to a local hospital. X-rays showed broken ribs on both sides of the seatbelt and broken vertebrae in my upper back. Even though I had lots of broken bones, they wouldn't keep me overnight. I was given pain pills and sent, via cab, to a Taco Bell and then a motel. I was heartbroken that my van was totaled, and now I was in a lot of pain.

The next day, the vet brought my dog to me. She had bruises but was walking normally. The sweet vet would not let me pay him. Later I sent him steaks. All the furniture and the dog crate had been bungeed down. Hubby arrived from our new home with a rental van and a lot of pillows. We returned to Roswell where I slowly recovered.

A year later we finally sold our home in Roswell. We were to close in two months, when—oh, no—another of life's unexpected moments. I had to have my appendix removed. A month later I had gall bladder surgery.

Life can be tough but I feel you have a choice to do everything to get well—or bore yourself, family and friends with your "pity party." I try very hard not to have pity parties but sometimes not hard enough.

Fast-forward eighteen years, after having a good report on my bone density. A few weeks later, I broke another vertebra in my lower back. It took weeks before surgery. I was absolutely miserable and, I am sorry to say, had a pity party for weeks. In addition there was severe arthritis in my lower spine. With surgery, some pain pills, heating pads and therapy, I got better. My M.D. told me later many people get over this type of injury without surgery. Apparently I feel pain more than most—lucky me.

The bad part is that I missed an entire summer in North Carolina. In spite of still having pain and therapy, we had to drive over five hundred miles to clean out our North Carolina home. A lot of decisions had to be made as we were moving once again.

We are now back to a normal life with me off the cane I had when I went to North Carolina. Therapy is complete and I am back to writing and getting on with my life. No time for pity parties!

P.S. Three years later we still have lots of books, furniture and stuff in storage.

P.P.S. Five years later we have the storage emptied and lots of stuff to put away. I feel guilty about the cost of moving and storing it.

Fun Being Silent

Over the last five years Hubby has lost a lot of his hearing. I have been told by other family members that I talk too loud. (Not easy being me.) When Hubby told me his doctor told him of his hearing loss five years ago, I agreed. Of course he didn't do anything. Engineers can be very, very, very stubborn! (Or so I hear.)

As time went by, I just talked louder. I noticed "the problem" was getting worse and worse, and I found myself getting more and more frustrated and more and more irritated! Get the picture? When he would ask me what I said, I would get louder and louder. Then he would say, "Don't scream at me." I'm sure it has not been easy for him and really not *fun* for me.

So where oh where is the fun here? Well, I have to tell you I like to learn new stuff and, yes, I find learning *fun*. Don't you?

Back to the story ... Hubby asked me what I wanted for Christmas. I told him I wanted him to get a hearing aid. It is hard to believe, but he did ask my "Dr. Four Eyes" to recommend a good hearing specialist. He did not want to go to Costco, where I have heard from several people hearing aids are a lot less expensive. Hubby wanted to go to a *real* doctor.

Off we went to Dr. Recommended (a Mayo "has-been"— meaning he left Mayo to go off on his own, be his own boss, etc.). Dr. Recommended did Hubby's hearing test. He showed Hubby the print-out— showing a big loss in the left ear and, yes, significant loss in the right. The doctor contacted another doctor to make sure "nothing else" was going on. I was thinking, maybe a brain tumor, because I had a friend who had two brain surgeries and it turned out to be just hearing loss, thank God!

Let me tell you, this saved my sanity (whatever I have left) and our marriage. I was ready to divorce him—probably not, but life together was getting really, really, really tough! I'm not sure what the hearing aids cost, but I would have sacrificed a lot to pay twice as much. They are a blessing! Thank you, God again!

P.S. Speaking of ears, I'm tired of getting pimples in mine. Ever have that happen? For better or worse, really?

Fun at a Mountain Villa

We had rented a lovely two-bedroom two-bath villa in Franklin, North Carolina. The bedrooms were separated by the living/dining area, which contained an interesting rustic rock fireplace topped with a thick wooden mantel. Over it hung an oil painting of a red cardinal. Every wall had interesting original art. I became quite fond of a pair of rustic old red trucks in distressed frames.

A sofa, loveseat and chair were upholstered in a tobacco-colored leather. On each were attractive red pillows. The end and coffee tables were a dark stained oak. At one end of the sofa sat an attractive small wood-topped iron-legged table. An oak reproduction of an 1800s three-drawer dresser sat under the wide-screen television. Loads of accessories everywhere, a large eagle, a ceramic owl, metal containers with dry weeds, a large silk plant, a couple of photos of grandkids and a ceramic basket maybe used as a wastebasket, not sure.

The dining area had an 1800s reproduction round oak table with matching spindle-backed chairs. Ceramic apples were placed in a beautiful, hand-rubbed wooden bowl on the lazy susan. On the small side wall was a tiny table made from an old sewing machine, which Hubby took over as his computer desk. To the right of the dining area was a Pullman kitchen with dark stained cabinets with interesting, perhaps handmade, dark olive tile counters full of, yes, more accessories.

The very dark stained wood floors were covered in the

living area and hallway to the second bedroom with very contemporary oval swirl design of light beige, tan, light and dark brown. The window treatments were custom valances, a bit dressy for this room. The walls were painted a pale gray with white woodwork. Sliding doors off the living area led to an attractive long narrow porch with an awesome view of the mountains. The leaves of the trees were beginning to change color when we were leaving, three weeks later.

The porch had two wrought iron black-finished chairs with a matching love loveseat, all having olive green cushions. A round thirty-inch metal table with two artsy-fartsy aluminum folding chairs provided a place for a casual meal. Beyond the porch was a brick patio with a nice bench to gaze out on God's wonderful creations. The porch too had interesting artwork hanging on the wall with a wooden sign that said, "My Happy Place."

On either side of the living area were the two bedrooms and baths, plus more original art and a print or two. The guest room I slept in had two double beds, complete with white eyelet dust skirts topped with printed calico bedspreads, plus more pillows. Between the beds was an antique oak table with a large ceramic lamp. Large, square woven baskets hung over the beds on the light yellow wall. An antique oak dresser with an attached beveled mirror sat in the corner; an old trunk was nearby. The adjoining bath had a large vanity with wall-covering mirror above. Beyond the vanity was a toilet and tub shower. A door led to a small hall closet with a washer and dryer behind louvered doors; beyond was the living area.

On the other side of the living room was a large master with a similar bath except this one had a walk-in shower. This large bedroom had a huge red barn painting over the bed as well as more artwork and accessories everywhere. One wall held a large television. A large maple dresser with a mirror matched the end tables. Beyond were sliding doors on to the porch.

Attractive lamps were placed throughout the villa. While most of the accessories were handcrafted and no doubt valuable and collected over time, there were just too many. We moved a lot of them so we could put a newspaper, book or anything down. While I love, love, love accessories, I was overwhelmed. It made me aware of the power of editing. Maybe the owner and I need to change them out.

The lovely mountain view made this place special. The single-lane road with blind curves was not fun. We appreciated how clean this place was and loved it being only seven miles from Franklin.

Fun with Obituaries

I love reading OBs! So far, none are about me. A friend of mine and I talk about the unusual ones and some of the interesting people we wish we had met. We love how creative or funny some of them seem.

Most OBs today are traditional, with "passed away" being the favorite phrase. As people have to pay for OBs by the word, wouldn't "died" work? We notice "suddenly taken from us"—interesting, but makes us wonder how and why, right? Love this one: "transcended to the church triumphant." Also like "returned to his heavenly home." Say, how do you know that?

A favorite one mentioned that he would be missed by his pet pig, whatever her name was.

But my all-time very favorite was for a former naval officer who "sailed away to the great beyond."

I saw these a few years ago, but still find them amusing. Maybe my friend and I have a screw or two loose. Think so?

Fun with Love and Heartbreak

Heartbreaks are hell, I know. Years ago, my now husband came to Dayton, Ohio, to see his mom and me. When he was ready to leave, he told me he had my ring but wasn't ready to give it to me. I said, "You date others, as I certainly intend to."

Soon I was going out with my previous steady and also had a couple of fun dates with a guy I met through work. No, that did not mean I was fickle, it meant I was going to try to continue to have fun with gals and guys in my age range. I continued to write Mr. Hoover, but most of my non-working thoughts would *not* be about him.

Sidebar: My mother was concerned about the wedding gown I had in lay-away. I told her if I didn't get to use it when marrying Mr. Hoover, I would save it for another guy. (We had broken up twice before.)

I might never see him again, but I was having a good time with his mom. When I wrote Mr. Hoover, I told him where I had gone on a date, never telling him who I went with. I later found out he only went out once with a secretary from work. He just wasn't ready for marriage. (Timing is everything. This was in the days when nice girls didn't have sex before marriage.)

Honestly, young ones, as Shakespeare, I believe, said, "True love never runs smoothly"—or some such thing. I think you have to pray for the "right person," *not* just any certain guy. Maybe God has someone *more special* planned for you. Dry up those tears and have some fun *every* day.

Today I feel it would be very difficult to have someone break your heart as you probably have had sex. Another reason, sweetie, to wait awhile. Tell guys you want to get to know them first. If they don't want to get to know you—so be it. I read where guys think about sex every seven minutes. You need to know most men view sex as a release, a moment of joy, whereas women become emotional and thus sex becomes an act of bonding. Guys will tell you they love you when they don't even know you, anything for a conquest. *No, life isn't fair.* (Keep in mind, guys mature slower than gals, thus aren't usually mature mentally until about age twenty-seven.)

I have a younger, fifty-five-year-old widow friend who met a really attractive guy on the beach. After dating awhile, my very sweet and pretty friend invited him to fly to New Orleans for a long weekend. The next morning, she came out of the shower and he asked her if she had gotten his text. He had broken up with her in a text while she was in the shower. Ugh. He insisted *she* rent a car and that they drive back to our island. Get this, they didn't even talk at all during the five-hour journey home. (FYI, I would have asked the SOB why he was acting like a jerk.) This was extremely hard on her.

About nine months later my pretty friend gave me a call and said she had met a local guy she found interesting. When she told me his name I said, "I know him, as about twenty years ago he took care of our yard."

"Really? What did you think of him?" she asked.

Not knowing they had already moved in together, I told her I really didn't get to know him before he got a much higher-paying job in Jacksonville and I had not seen him since. A week later she invited me over to see her newly remodeled beach home. He was there and busy doing some yard work. We had a brief conversation. Let's just say the years hadn't been super-kind to him. Their relationship moved very quickly and soon he was talking marriage. I, as her friend, was feeling a bit protective and questioned the timing. He introduced her to his relatives. They loved her as much as I do. She took him to meet some of her relatives and apparently, they liked him too.

They were planning a trip to Africa, and when they went to the courthouse to get passport information, he said to her, "We might as well get our marriage license."

On the way home my friend said, "You really haven't asked me to marry you." He laughed and said something like, "You're right."

The next morning, he went out to do errands and when he came home said, "You have to come with me *now*, it's important!" They crossed the road to the beach and written in the sand was, "Will you marry me?" Wasn't this the most romantic moment? They were married a couple of weeks later in a private ceremony.

I hear he does the grocery shopping and most of the cooking. Wow! So far, so good. I only hope he doesn't take advantage of her financially or any other way, or as I told him, "If you aren't sweet to her, I'll just have to come over and rip your eyes out." I am protective and supportive of all my girlfriends.

Jenna Bush Hager told an unbelievable break-up story she experienced. She brought groceries and arrived at her boyfriend's place to fix him dinner. The jerk broke up with her while she stood there on the porch holding the groceries.

Maybe these girls had to experience heartbreaks to find and appreciate the good guys they married. Most everyone I know has experienced a break-up or two. Some girls become sluts as they are so desperate for attention and what they *think* is love. They think they will feel better about themselves if a guy *wants them*. In most cases it is about the guy's physical needs—beware. Often after a breakup, the guy moves on in a day or two. If you broke up with him, it may be an act of revenge. Remember, every seven minutes, guys are thinking sex, sex, sex!

To my sweet young virgins—do value yourself and your body enough that you have the courage to say "no" or "not yet." And please, please, please use protection. I suggest you go on double dates with like-minded sister-friends. *Always* have money for a ride home. Let friends know where you are going and with whom. Order a can of Coke or one beer, sip on it, and take it with you to the ladies' room to avoid someone trying to put a mind-blowing drug into your drink. *Think!* Notice how much your date and friends are drinking. If you feel *uncomfortable,* call for a ride home. *Do not take chances*! Every time you get into a car with a drunk driver you are risking your life. *Keep safe.* I need my readers!

P.P.S. There are nice, intelligent, caring guys. But they may be hiding.

Fun with the Carters

July 24 , 2019
Dear Mr. Jimmy Carter,
Happy Belated Birthday, Mr. President!

Enclosed is a ROUGH draft of a chapter from my upcoming third fun book. I thought you might enjoy reading about my friendship with your Aunt Sissy.

We moved from Roswell to Amelia Island twenty-one years ago.

Hope this finds you and your family doing well.
Sincerely,
Emily J. Hoover

(Sadly, I never heard back from Mr. Carter.)

Sometimes I meet really interesting or unusual people

because I love people! Because my Hubby was an electrical microwave engineer, I have come to know a lot of his working buddies. As you know, I like to joke around and, yes, maybe see if they have some retorts for me. Okay, sometimes these brilliant guys are so shocked at what I say they are speechless.

In Atlanta I was chosen to head the women's program for the IEEE International Microwave Symposium. The local guys knew I had been co-chairman of the women's program in Clearwater, Florida, and also one in Palo Alto, California. This time I was the chairman. I forget where all I took the group, but I remember taking them to the Georgia Governor's Mansion.

I asked the guard if Jimmy was in. He told me unfortunately, he was not! This really nice guy told me Jimmy's Aunt Sissy, Rosalynn and Amy were there that day. As we went up the steps this round-faced fun-looking lady says, "Hi, welcome to the Governor's Mansion. I am Jimmy's Aunt Sissy." (His mother's youngest sister.) When I introduced myself and told her I lived in Roswell, Georgia, she said, "Emily, that is my given name and I live in Roswell."

When the gals were getting ready to leave, Aunt Sissy said, "If you should see Jimmy's name on the ballot for president, I'm asking you right now for your vote." I'll never forget her sweet, but oh so feisty, Southern voice.

As I was checking around for stray people preparing to leave, Rosalynn and six-year-old Amy (in a cowgirl outfit) descended the stairs. Rosalynn introduced herself to me. What a beautiful woman with porcelain skin and a very tiny waist. (I knew she had had five children.) I told her I had heard Jimmy might run for president and wondered if she would like to go out to the bus and say hello to my travelers. As shy as she seemed, she did come out and speak briefly to our group.

Roswell probably had around 12,000 to 15,000 people at the time. I often would run into Aunt Sissy as I did my errands and we would chat for a few minutes. She lived on a historic street in an always immaculate, white Victorian home with a wide wrap-around front porch.

I ran into her one day after she had been down to Plains for Jimmy's launch of his book *An Hour Before Dawn*. It is about his life growing up on the farm, milking cows by hand in the mud—ugh. I told her I saw Jimmy on TV earlier in the day. I also told her she looked better than Jimmy. She laughed and said, "I can't wait to tell him."

When I ran into her another time, she introduced me to her handsome new husband. She told me that they had made a deal. He didn't have to do yard work and she didn't have to cook. She went on to say she was going to have a part-time cook and go out to eat (sounds like a good deal to me.) I asked Aunt Sissy to come speak to our American Association of University Women's group. She was awesome; however, due to a rare Atlanta snowstorm, we had to adjourn early. I don't remember much of what she said, other than in the 1940s she and others delivered rat poison to Roswell homes to rid the town of the pests.

I would have loved to meet President Carter. I believe he studied engineering of some kind while at the Naval Academy. His mom, Lillian, was something else. She was born in 1898 and was trained in nursing, apparently caring for people most of her life. In her seventies, she went to help out in the Peace Corps. I'll bet Lillian was a fascinating lady. I wish I could have met her as I found her book, *Miss Lillian and Friends, The Plains, Georgia, Family Philosophy and Recipe Book,* very interesting.

P. S. Our family saw President Carter's limo go down West Crossville and Holcomb Bridge Road in front of our home, about seventy feet from where we stood. We waved as he drove by.

Fun and Not So Fun in 2020

After a nice family Christmas with our eldest and my daughter-in-love, we were soon swept into 2020.

After a lot of pain starting in late October 2019, I was finally scheduled for minor back surgery—the end of February, after my eighty-fifth birthday on February 24. I had not seen our youngest or our grandson for almost a year, and we were really looking forward to our family get-together. Sadly, due to job commitments, our grandson and his wife were unable to come. It became my worst birthday ever, as I was unable to sit at the dining room table. Our daughter-in-love and sons prepared a wonderful meal that we ate on our laps. They gave me lovely and thoughtful gifts; however, I couldn't wait for them to leave. I couldn't get up from my bed or chair without crying.

This came about, I believe, from overdoing and painting three end tables plus a few more projects. When I was hurting, I took more Advil and kept on going. I should have taken a couple of days off. Apparently, a vertebra broke. Dumb, dumb me! If you have back issues or back pain, you really need to pace yourself—I didn't. This was the second time that overdoing it did me in!

After minor surgery and rest, I was feeling better and ready to get out of the house when the COVID global pandemic hit! I truly believe if government officials had taken it seriously in the very beginning, thousands of lives could have been saved. Instead, unfortunately, it became political and very nasty. This is never good! Hubby took up grocery shopping when I could not go, but when I was ready to, he didn't want me to go. He said I talk too much to too many people, and he didn't want me to get the virus and give it to him. What can I say? I love people and live in a small town, and I usually run into three or four people I know every time I go out.

During 2020, I lost twelve people I knew. Two were from COVID in our small neighborhood.

Finding their photos in the local paper was overwhelmingly sad. One of them, Helen Eisile, was a gal I had known in Clearwater in the 1950s. Our kids were in kindergarten together, she and I belonged to AAUW, and both our families attended the Methodist church. After we moved to California in 1965, we exchanged Christmas cards. Sometime later we lost touch. Several months ago, reading the obituaries, I saw her name and photo and that she lived on our island, about a mile away. I didn't even know she lived here. How super-sad! She was a bright, beautiful, fun gal.

Another friend of Helen and mine was Jane Alison, who had died shortly before Helen. Jane and I were asked to go to the Pinellas School Board in the early 1960s, where Jane made a presentation to get kindergarten and Head Start curriculum into the county school system. (At the time unless you could provide transportation and the fees to pay for kindergarten, your child would go straight into the first grade.) Later she was very active in goody-good projects in Bryson City, North Carolina. Jane helped raise funds and helped to design a new senior center. Her daughter-in-law told me that Jane was living there for a month or two before she died and was going downhill mentally. She had joked telling her family and friends that she "ran the whole place." My biggest regret is that I forgot to send her a birthday card in July for her ninetieth birthday and that I had not called her more often. She really was like an older sister to me.

Learn from my mistakes and keep up with your friends! Thank God I have made an effort in later years to gain some younger friends. I am truly grateful that although losing so many precious people, I still have many friends who keep in touch with me. Thank you, God, as friends have always been very important to me.

During the stress of 2020, I became addicted to TV, worked on this, my third book, and managed to read a couple of books and, unfortunately, lots of magazines and catalogs.

Frankly, I'm just happy most of us made it through the deaths, elections, and hopefully beginning to see the end of COVID.

In 2021, I hope to finish this book, complete my decorating book, keep my hair cut and colored. (I used to joke and say, "I'll be bleaching my hair until I'm eighty-five." Guess what? I still have some dark roots.) However, at eighty-six, I am happy I am still walking, talking, and giving doctors a rough time. I would really like to go to North Carolina for a month. Here's hoping. I am anxious to do book signings, seeing old friends and making new ones. I want to take up painting again. As our home is almost twenty-five years old, it needs some touch-ups and new decorating. First, I am going to clean out the clutter, and, oh, God, do I need your help!

Did I mention that I lost thirty pounds? How? By cutting portions, not eating after 8 p.m. at night, having brunch at 10 or 11 a.m., a light snack with a glass of wine around 5 p.m. and a light dinner at 7 p.m. I eat pretty much what I want, just less of it. I exercise every day, about twenty to thirty minutes, and walk around the neighborhood (probably three to three and a half blocks) or go up and down the stairs several times. My much younger sister did not exercise and she ended up bedridden and dying at seventy-four of heart-related problems, as did our brother and parents. About thirty years ago, I was advised by my health-conscious dentist to take the supplement CoQ10, now called Ubiquinol. I am not on any heart medications but do take a baby aspirin along with a handful of supplements daily.

Every day we all make choices. Much as I hate exercise, I do it every day! I have had many surgeries and have felt like giving up but chose not to. I know that keeping in good mental health is important too and getting people to laugh helps me.

Nothing pleases me more than shocking people (who probably don't give a damn about me) when they ask, "How are you today?" and I say," Not bad for an old bitch." People will either laugh or look disgusted—either way, it is interesting.

What makes you happy? I love watching some of the TV and Netflix shows. Which ones do you like? I tend toward the house decorating shows or comedies. When I have time, I also love to read. I just finished reading *Amelia Island's Golden Years, Silver Tears* (a historical novel) by Maggie Carter-DeVries, and *The Wonder Boy of Whistle Stop* by my favorite author, Fannie Flagg; she also wrote *Fried Green Tomatoes*, which was made into a movie. Then I hope to read *Hissy Fit* by another favorite author, Mary Kay Andrews. I favor Southern writers for their wonderful, colorful characters.

We all need to thank God for getting us through 2020 (and then through 2021!) and for all the gifts we get from God each and every day.

Hope to meet you soon at a book signing.

May God bless you and yours!

P.S. Good news! My P.A. told me people can take MiraLAX every day, as it won't hurt us. Recently I received nine catalogs, and on the front of one it said, in green caps:

Relief M.D. In white letters below, "Doctors call it GUT MUD." The entire catalog was for probiotics, stating, "You don't poop, you don't pay!" It also says, "We rush so you can flush!" If need be, you can send your check made to Green Valley Natural Solutions. Made in the good old USA! Maybe you could have a crappy but good day. Ha-ha!

Some say I have a weird sense of humor—you think?

Fun Writing

So, you think writing is fun? So, you want to write a book and want to know how to begin? I can only tell you what I have experienced. I write my books by hand as I am not a good typist. I pass my chapters to my trusty typist friend who types, retypes and retypes several times. Then it is sent to my editor. She checks it over, making notes for me to work on to keep me from looking like a real idiot. Next, I have someone send it to a self-publishing firm. This can mean several proofs before I finally say, "Print it."

I selected the self-publishing route due to several factors: 1, more control; 2, much quicker turnaround; 3, my lack of patience; and 4, I know main-line publishers want to get at least three books out of an author in order to make any money.

I hear that some well-known writers are going to self-publishing as they like the faster turnaround and make more money. Unless you have a huge following of a million or more, there is very little money, if any, to be made writing books. My books sell for about fifteen dollars. The bookstore gets about five dollars. When I do book signings in a bookstore, I get ten dollars back but have paid eight and a half dollars to have it printed. Note: This does not count the countless hours I have spent writing and rewriting, or typing and editing costs. Then, unless the author has a huge following, bookstores don't want to have self-published books on the shelves.

Most of the time, I sell eight to ten books at a signing if I am blessed. Twelve to fifteen dollars is hardly worth all the effort unless you are doing it for fun and love meeting people. No matter how well you write, and I am sure most of you are better writers than I am, you still have to *sell your product*. If you are shy or can't take rejection, you might want to spend your time doing something fun. If you weren't an English major in college, you may feel out of place and out-classed. It could drive you crazy. I am a perfect example of trying to do something out of my comfort zone; however, I whine less about the writing when I have had a glass of wine! Ha!

A few more personal tips:

1. You either have to love writing, or you have to be driven to do it.

2. If you write a page a day, in a year you'll have written a book.

3. You will do better if you have a writing friend or life coach to help motivate you to keep going.

4. You *absolutely* need a good editor.

5. Hopefully you have a lot of patience, or you'll be very frustrated with all the rewriting and the publishing process. I feel it is a nightmare.

6. *Do not* expect family members or friends to be excited about your book.

7. You have to believe in what you are doing.

8. Try to go to writer conferences and book festivals to learn all you can about writing.

9. Read and study how to market your book.

10. I challenge you to start by keeping a journal. *Do it*

now!

Advice from two professional writers: Pulitzer-winning author Richard Russo said in his book *One Destiny Thief*, "Writing, like life itself, is difficult. Many truly talented people give up every day." Ernest Hemingway states in *A Moveable Feast* that sometimes when writing he had a problem getting started. At this point he would say to himself, "All you have to do is write one true sentence. Write the truest sentence you know."

Now, what others have said: Amy Poehler says in her book, *Yes, Please*, "The truth is this: writing is hard and boring... like hacking away at a freezer with a screwdriver." I agree.

An English professor at Mercer University said this: "Choose a subject you know, do not be trite and be sure that your descriptions are vivid." (*Atlanta Journal-Constitution*, September 1, 2006.) This man had inspired Dr. Ferrol Sams, the physician who wrote *Run With the Horsemen*. Dr. Sams got up at 4:30 a.m. to write before seeing his patients in Fayetteville, Georgia. Dr. Sams wrote his book by hand (like I do.) His book was chosen by 2006 Atlanta Reads, a community reading program. In a *Journal-Constitution* article, Dr. Sams said, "You either like to write or you don't like to write.... Yes, writing is work." Then he asked, "What have you accomplished in your lifetime that was worth a damn that was easy?"

I love meeting people at book signings or Silver Sneakers, restaurants, doctors' offices, airports, on planes or just about anywhere. I love people! I find all sorts of people fun and very few not so much. Those people usually see me coming and move out of my way, Yes, I get it. Not everyone likes a big-mouthed, bad-ass old bitch. But guess what? There are a good many that tell me I made their day, or grin and hug me. Most nurses seem to appreciate my sense of humor. Hint, hint,

hint—any of my books make a good gift for any nurse angel. With what they have to deal with on a daily basis, they certainly deserve a laugh or two, don't you think?

So, don't tell me you have thought about writing a book; just do it, or forget it. The decision is up to you. If I, not a talented person, can do it, you can too!

Now, on to complete *Decorating Isn't a Joke, Or Is It?* This is a book I am having fun writing but hasn't come out yet. I have sketches, photographs and a bit more research to finish. Hope to have it out before my next birthday.

Fun with God, Goodness, and Gratefulness

For sure, God has issues with me. Well, God, I have a lot of unanswered questions for you. For instance, why do some people have so much trouble forgiving each other—especially if they have been longtime friends? Why are seemingly good people sometimes victims of horrible crimes? Why are there so many wars and so much violence in our world?

God, couldn't you have made all people more attractive? Hey, especially me? God, it's a joke—I know you could have done worse with me. But maybe you could have given me a better brain, a thinner butt and better stomach muscles. And, God, why do I have so much trouble thinking things through *before* I open my mouth? You know in my heart I wouldn't do anything to hurt *anyone*, except roaches—then I go into killer mode.

God, I gotta say, I'm not happy with your giving us crap with our bodies just when we "figure life out." Why? I ask you, who needs brittle bones, memory loss, failing eyesight, and the biggie—losing loved ones and longtime friends?

And, God, why do guys lose their brains, divorce their longtime partners and cause so much hurt for their families while chasing much younger women?

I know guys don't have it easy. It seems the hair on their heads slips to their eyebrows, then it comes out of their ears and noses. And what happens to their waists? Doesn't it say in Genesis 1:26 that man was made in your image?

And, God—what about those sex enhancement drugs? Who needs to go on for hours and hours? I've heard of old men dying of heart attacks while having sex, often with someone other than their wife. It isn't fair to their families.

Hey, God, women have had enough trouble. No man I have talked to wants to come back as a woman. (Except Bruce Jenner—and I have heard Caitlyn complain about how much trouble being a woman is.) Come on, I was in a state of shock as I grew up and, yes, irritation from cramps and my period. Why make us "bitchy" every month? And, God, for your information, childbirth is horrible. And, God, as cute as they *can* be, children aren't that easy to raise. Guess who has the most responsibility for their day-to-day care?

And, God, what's with our teenagers? Aren't pimples and emotional difficulties enough without making them act so stupid at times? It is bad enough that they can't reason properly until they are almost thirty. God, did you have to make most of them "know-it-alls?" (I'm truly sorry, but I have lots and lots of questions for you, "big guy.")

Yes, God, I read your book. (Question, have you read mine? Of course not. You're very busy.) Yes, I read Genesis 1:24, where it says God said, "Let the land yield all kinds of living things, cattle and creeping things and wild beasts of every sort, and so it was done." Hey, I still think you took creepy things way too far. But, hey, what do I know? I do *not* understand your planning roaches or armadillos, warthogs, rhinos, mice, rats, and ratfink people.

But, God, I realize I am blessed to have a lot to be

grateful for in my life:
- I am grateful that you forgive me when others may not.
- I am grateful I have learned to forgive, and as you know, it hasn't been easy for me.
- I am grateful for my loving parents, even though Mother was verbally a bit rough on me.
- I am grateful for my grandparents, who all seemed to think I was special as I was their first grandchild. (They soon learned I wasn't so special after more were born.)
- I am grateful for my loving, mostly patient and kind Hubby.
- I am grateful for my oldest son and how he is like his Dad in so many wonderful ways.
- I am grateful for his beautiful wife. I realize you could never have given a more loving daughter.
- I am grateful for my youngest son. I appreciate your calling him to help those going to meet their maker. (For several years, he worked as a chaplain for Hospice.)
- I am very grateful for his sweet and loving partner of almost thirty years.
- I am grateful for my adorable loving grandson.
- I am grateful for my loving granddaughter-in-law, a gal we all adore.
- I am grateful for all the people who love me in spite of my not always being lovable.
- I am ever grateful for all my caring friends, whom I love.
- I am grateful for my health professionals and for my vitamins, herbs and medicines that keep me going.
- I am grateful for our nice, comfortable home and the funds to keep it up.
- I am grateful for a good bed, pillow, clean sheets and warm blankets, for air conditioning and heat as needed.

- I am grateful for my sweet neighbors.
- I am very grateful for "Lipstick," my then-new 2016 metallic red Ford Escape, and my limited inheritance that is helping to pay for it.
- I am grateful that you inspire me to be creative in my art, writing, decorating and my humor.
- I am so grateful for my special readers who have expressed their enjoyment in reading and laughing at the stuff I write.
- I am grateful for all the life lessons I've learned from all the crappy things that have happened to me. (I read somewhere that when crap happens to you, you need to ask yourself what God is trying to teach you.)
- I will be even more grateful if you would quit teaching me.
- I am grateful for all the wonderful events and opportunities you have given me.
- I am so grateful for all the sweet, loving, beautiful Dalmatians I have whelped or helped to plan that have brought happiness to others and me.
- I am always grateful for good steaks, wonderful salads, baked sweet potatoes, a glass or two of white wine, Becky's carrot cake, chocolate cake with fudge icing and great vanilla ice cream. And yes
- I am also grateful for milk chocolate candy with almonds, pulled pork, cole slaw, fresh sliced tomatoes, and fresh corn on the cob.
- I am even more grateful if someone else fixes my food.
- I am grateful that I didn't grow up super-ugly, although I went through ugly stages.
- I am grateful for make-up, hair color, nice clothes, and the ability to keep up my appearance.
- I am grateful for gentle rain, warm weather and sunny

skies, trees, grass, and those beautiful flowers and plants.
- Finally, I am grateful for every little thing I have ever been given in my life.
- I am grateful I am never alone as I always feel God is with me.
- I am grateful that I found Florence Scovel Shinn's book *The Wisdom of Florence Scovel Shinn,* as she has inspired so many ministers and taught me through her books the power of affirmations, forgiveness, and the power of being grateful.

Fun with More Recipes

Fun Rum Punch

(Try saying this fast, five times after having one.)

9 oz. rum
9 oz. orange juice
3 oz. Ruby Red grapefruit juice
6 oz. cranberry juice

Shake with ice, then strain into snifter glasses over ice cubes. Garnish with sugar-coated cranberries.

***

Pink Grapefruit Margaritas

5 oz. pink grapefruit juice (fresh is best!)
½ oz. agave or simple syrup
4 oz. tequila
White sugar or margarita salt for rims
1½ oz. Triple Sec
Slices of grapefruit quartered for garnish

Place all liquids into a cocktail shaker filled with ice. Shake vigorously then pour over ice into sugar-rimmed glasses. Finish with a pink grapefruit garnish. Enjoy!

***

Holiday Spiced Pecans

¼ c. sugar
¼ t. cinnamon
1/8 t. dried cloves
1 c. chopped pecans
¼ t. dried ginger

Combine sugar, spices and pecans into a saucepan. Stir over medium heat until sugar melts. Spread out on a parchment-lined cookie sheet. Cool, stir, then serve in a decorative bowl.

***

Cherry-Cranberry Sauce

1 pkg. (12 oz.) fresh or frozen cranberries
½ c. dried chopped cherries
1/3 c. red wine
1 c. sugar
1 red apple, cored and cut into chunks

Combine cranberries, sugar, cherries and wine in pot over medium/high heat. After bringing to a boil, reduce to low and cook until cranberries burst and mixture has thickened, about ten minutes. Transfer mixture to heatproof bowl and stir in apple. Cool and refrigerate until ready to serve.

***

Chinese Coleslaw

1 lb. finely shredded cabbage
1 cup hickory smoked almonds
4 sliced green onions
¼ c. oil

1 (3-oz.) pkg. chicken-flavored ramen noodles
½ c. roasted and salted sunflower seeds
2 T. cider vinegar
¼ c sugar or Splenda

In a large bowl, combine cabbage, broken-up noodles, almonds, sunflower seeds and onion. Set aside.
In a small bowl, whisk together the contents of the ramen flavor packet, vinegar, oil and sugar/Splenda. When mixed, pour over the cabbage mixture. Mix well and serve at once.

***

Southern Sweet Potato Salad

2 c. cooked and cubed sweet potatoes   1 c. cubed apple
1 c. orange sections cut into chunks   1 c. diced celery
1 c. mayo (more to taste)
¼ c. chopped nuts if desired

Mix cubed and diced ingredients with mayo, fold in sweet potatoes. Chill before serving.

***

Morning Sausage Muffins

1 link uncooked German sausage   3 eggs
1 c. plus 3 T. flour   2 tsp. baking powder
Pinch each of salt and pepper   ½ c. milk
1 ½ c. grated Cheddar cheese   3 T. olive oil

Preheat oven to 350 degrees. In bowl, combine eggs, oil and milk. In separate bowl, mix flour, baking powder, salt and pepper. Add egg mixture to flour mixture and stir to combine. Slice sausage lengthwise, and scrape meat filling into batter. Discard casing. Stir cheese into batter. Pour into greased muffin cups. Bake 18 to 20 minutes. Makes nine muffins.

Bill's Barbeque Sauce

1 6-oz. can tomato paste
½ c. Worcestershire sauce
1/3 c. molasses
1 finely minced onion
2 T. celery salt
1 T. liquid smoke

3 c. cider vinegar
1.5 t. brown sugar
2 t. paprika
1 T. ground black pepper
2 T. granulated garlic

Mix all ingredients together in a saucepan. Bring to a boil; reduce heat and let simmer for two hours.

***

Ann's Garlic and Lemon Chicken with Red Potatoes and Green Beans

2 lemons: one thinly sliced, one juiced
8 small red potatoes, quartered
4 chicken breasts
¾ lb. green beans
4 cloves minced garlic
6 T. olive oil
1 T. salt
½ T. freshly ground pepper

Preheat oven to 400 degrees. Coat a large baking dish with one tablespoon of the olive oil. Arrange the lemon slices in a single layer in the bottom of the dish. In a large bowl, combine the remaining oil, lemon juice, garlic, salt and pepper. Add the chicken, green beans and potatoes, and toss to coat. Pour this mixture into the baking dish and spread around evenly. Roast for 400 degrees until cooked through. Serve warm.

***

Hubby's Butterbeans and Sausage

One link mild Italian sausage, precooked
1 can large butterbeans, drained
1/3 to ½ diced onion   3 cloves minced garlic
1 can diced tomatoes   Approx. ½ glass red wine
Salt, to taste

Combine drained butterbeans and diced tomatoes in a saucepan. Heat on medium. Add onions and garlic. Slice precooked sausage into bite-size pieces and add to saucepan. Add wine to make sufficient liquid. Bring pot to a low simmer for about 30 minutes.

***

Emily's Favorite Harvest Ham Supper

6 carrots, sliced in half lengthwise
3 sweet potatoes, sliced in half lengthwise
1 ½ lbs. boneless ham   1 c. maple syrup

Place carrots and potatoes in bottom of a slow cooker to form a rack. Place ham on top of vegetables. Pour syrup to cover. (Emily likes to use ¾ c. of low-sugar syrup with ¼ c. of regular syrup.) Cover and cook on low for 6-8 hours. Enjoy! Good with cornbread and slaw or salad.

***

Judy's Easy Faux Apple Cobbler

2 cans apple pie filling
½ sleeve of crumbled graham crackers
¼ c. sugar   2 T. butter

Preheat oven to 350 degrees. Mix graham crumbs and sugar. Grease square glass baking pan. Pour in apples. Top with cracker/sugar mix. Dot with butter. Bake at 350 until bubbly.

Applesauce Cake

2 c. flour	2 t. baking soda
1 c. sugar	¼ t. cloves
1 t. salt	1 t. cinnamon
½ t. nutmeg	1 c. raisins
1 c. chopped walnuts	½ c. melted butter
1 large jar applesauce	Powdered sugar (optional)

Preheat oven to 350 degrees. Mix together all ingredients except powdered sugar. Beat until well blended. Pour into 9x9-inch pan or tube pan (well-greased). Bake at 350 degrees for 45 to 50 minutes. When cooled, sprinkle powdered sugar over top of cake. Enjoy.

Also, good warm with maybe a scoop of vanilla ice cream?

***

Raspberry Shortbread Bars

1 c. butter	1.5 c. confectioners' sugar
2 c. all-purpose flour	¾ t. salt
2 tsp. almond extract	½ c. seedless raspberry jam
¼ c. sliced almonds	

Preheat oven to 350 degrees. Line 9-inch baking pan with foil, leaving a 2-inch overhang, then grease. Cream butter and confectioners' sugar, and extract until fluffy. Gradually add flour and salt, and beat on low until well blended. After reserving ½ c. dough, press the rest on the bottom of the baking pan. Spread raspberry jam to within ½ inch of the edges. Crumble the reserved dough over the jam and top with almonds. Bake 45 minutes until golden brown. Cool in pan for 15 minutes. Using foil, transfer to wire rack to cool completely, then cut into bars. Makes 16 servings.

Book Club Discussion Questions

1. What was your favorite chapter? Why?
2. What made you laugh out loud?
3. What part of the book do you think was the most fun?
4. Did you learn anything new? What?
5. Would you like to hang out with Emily? Why? Why not?
6. Did you like the recipe chapter?
7. Have you tried any of the recipes? Results?
8. Would you enjoy reading Emily's next book on decorating? (It will be out in 2022, titled *Decorating Isn't a Joke, Or Is It*?)

Watch Emily's website for updates or check with Amazon for books available.

If you liked her book, **Emily would really appreciate a post on Amazon, Barnes and Noble, Lulu.com or other sites**.

For Amazon, you go to Amazon.com. In the search bar, type in the name of the book. Select the book and open the page so the book sales page is showing. Under the author's name will be an area that shows stars. Next to the stars it says, "Customer reviews." Click on that; it will give you an option to write a review and rate the book. Thank you!

Fun Information About Decorating Isn't a Joke, Or Is It?

Years ago Emily developed a course on decorating for the Florida Pinellas County Adult Program. She has decorated model homes for several builders while continuing to teach the adult interior design classes in Florida, California and Georgia. While in Georgia, she taught interior design, fashion classes and advertising to young adults at the Atlanta School of Art and Design.

Emily worked as a designer in Clearwater, Florida, for Classic Interiors and Perma House Interiors. In Atlanta she worked for Rich's and Davison's department stores. Later she had her own shop in Roswell, Georgia.

Now she is completing a fun do-it-yourself decorating book called *Decorating Isn't a Joke, Or Is It?* The book contains all the information you need for decorating your space from small college room to a very large home. It will give you wonderful ideas on how to freshen up your spaces, designer hints and decorator sources.

The book is written in a casual, fun, informative style and, yes, you may at times even laugh out loud.

If you want to know when it is released and how to obtain it, please send your email address to Emily at **emilyjoannehoover@gmail.com**, or you can check on Amazon.

Fun Decorating — Where to Start?

(A preview chapter from *Decorating Isn't a Joke, Or Is It?*)

Where to start? Maybe at the beginning. Ha, ha.

First, I believe you have to decide how much of your time, effort and money you want to invest. Ask yourself what you need and then what you want. Are you decorating a college room, your first apartment or retirement condo? Are you building your dream home, or perhaps you just want a fresh new look as you hold onto favorite things while updating your home? Regardless, this book can help you.

Your first consideration has to be the space you are decorating. This reminds me of a joke I heard years ago while working my way through The Ohio State University. God took a little string and made a little boy. He had a little left over, so He made a little thing. God took a little piece of lace and made a little girl. He didn't have enough, so He left a little space. Thank God.

Now, what are you going to do with your space? Think about how and when the space will be used. Why? Hey, a smart person doesn't put white carpet in a baby's room, right? Or a family room, unless you are like a former neighbor of mine who was a "super-clean" nurse. Their great room was used only by adults, but still …

What time of day will the room be used? How are the windows placed? What artificial light will you need? Do you prefer built-in lighting or portable lamps?

The size of the room and architectural elements need to be considered. I personally think that oversized furniture, a fad a few years back, belongs in larger rooms. If you have it and love it and need to keep it, do so. This will be a challenge in smaller rooms, but you can read how to make it work in this book.

You need to think of and plan for people who will be using the room. You want your family and friends to be comfortable. Do you plan to use the space for entertaining? How many people? The location of the room, the way the house flows, window views, need for privacy, and how and when the room is used are all important in decorating.

The personal styles of those using the space are to be taken into consideration in the selections that are made. What are your color preferences? Do you have furnishings on hand that you love or plan to use?

Design challenges will be addressed as you have fun reading this book. You will read about style and color and how to get "the look" you desire. I hope you find some things insightful. Perhaps you will look at your place in a new way.

When you least expect it, you may find something that will amuse you. You will learn more about the many interior design sources that are available today.

Enjoy!

Photos over the Years

Frank and Ada Zurbuch, Emily Hoover's maternal grandparents, mid-1900s

Below, Joseph Zurbuch, Emilys great-grandfather, who came from France

Zurbuch family: back row, L-R, Francis, Emily, Helen, Rose (author's mother); front, Ada, Dick, and Frank

Emily's father, in gown that Emily also wore for her christening

Emily's paternal grandparents

Emily's grandparents, her father and his younger brother

Ohio home where Emily and her father were born

At left, Emily, age 4, with parents and brother

Emily, at far right, with parents, brother, and little sister Gloria

Emily, age 11, with her champion Hampshire pig

Emily was Fayette County's Outstanding 4-H Girl of 1951.

At left, graduating from modeling school, in one of the dresses she made.

Below, Emily (top bunk, third from left) with OSU pals.

In band uniform, age 18, Mary Washington College

Wedding in 1958: Emily's parents at left, Emily and J.C., and his mother

30th birthday, Santa Clara, California

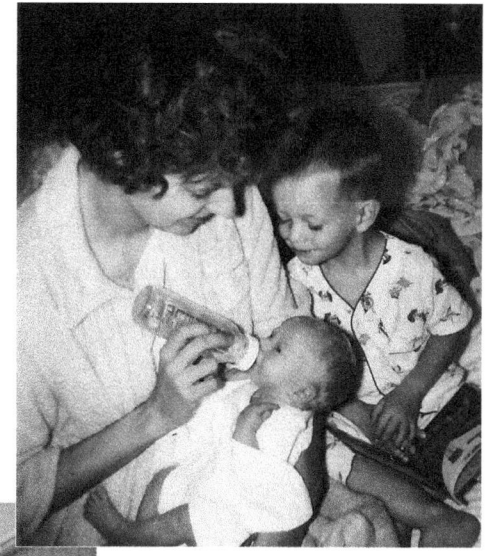

Emily with sons S.C., age 3, and T.J., newborn

At left, Emily in 1960 with her first car, a Fiat convertible

Hoover family, Easter 1964, at their Florida home

The Hoover boys

Friend Terri showing first-class winner at Dalmation Club of America; Emily is second from left.

Above, Emily at home with one of her Atlantis champions. At left, winning at a show with Champion Atlantis Flashdance.

Emily, center, with "Happi," the mama of all the other dogs in the photo. The puppies were a repeat breeding of Ch. Atlantis Love of Pacifica (far left). They were sired by the top winning dog Ch. Pacifica's Pride of Poseidon (Sy). Atlanta show 1967.

The Hoovers at an Atlanta family party in 1982. Below, invitation to their golden wedding anniversary celebration held in Franklin, N.C.

At left, Emily and J.C. with son T.J., grandson J.D., and J.C.s mother

At right, Emily's sister, Gloria, with her husband and sons

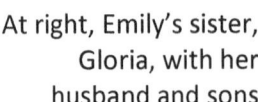

Wedding of oldest son, S.C.—from left, J.D., Emily, J.C., Becky, S.C., T.J., and R.M.

Hoover family home for 40 years in Roswell, Georgia

Grandson's wedding photo

Emily and her siblings with parents at an anniversary party

www.ingramcontent.com/pod-product-compliance
Lightning Source LLC
Chambersburg PA
CBHW060512090426
42735CB00011B/2187